Backyard Aluminum Casting

for Bike Shift Levers

(and Nearly Anything Else)

One Street Components

Publisher's Cataloging-in-Publication data
One Street Components.
Backyard aluminum casting for bike shift levers (and nearly anything else) / by One Street Components.
p. cm.
ISBN 978-0-9859889-1-3
Includes bibliographical references and index.

1. Aluminum alloys --Metallurgy. 2. Aluminum castings. 3. Bicycles --Design and construction. 4. Bicycles --Maintenance and repair. I. Title.

TA480.A6 O54 2014
620.1/86 --dc23 2014910424

Printed in the United States of America

First Edition

ISBN 978-0-9859889-1-3

One Street Press
P.O. Box 3309
Prescott, Arizona 86302
USA

www.onestreet.org

To everyone who contributed to the success of the Bike Shift Lever project and ultimately this book.

Table of Contents

Preface

About the Project

This book is for anyone interested in building a basic aluminum casting foundry. While much of this book discusses the Bike Shift Lever project, readers will discover how to cast just about anything using scrap aluminum and make a profit doing so. In addition to casting, the book also offers guidance on product marketing and sales.

One Street, founded in 2007, is an international nonprofit serving the needs of bicycle organizations all over the world. The Bike Shift Lever is the first project of One Street Components, a program we launched in 2012 in response to countless complaints from our partners about the rapid extinction of basic bicycle parts. Beyond designing and producing simple, affordable, durable, and repairable bike parts, we hope to inspire an expectation for such bikes and parts from other manufacturers. Bringing basic bikes and parts back into production will serve not only people struggling with poverty, but the vast majority of people who simply want to ride a bike without having to deal with high-tech gadgets or poor-quality parts. Racers are more than well served. It's time the rest of us had access to bike parts that we can use and repair with confidence.

Preface

Even a few years ago, One Street was happily focused on providing coaching, resources, and services to leaders of bicycle organizations as they worked to increase bicycling in their communities. One Street's mission is to serve the needs of these leaders. Most of our work involves planning for successful campaigns and managing effective organizations. Casting was the farthest thing from our minds.

While One Street serves all sorts of bicycle organizations, our flagship program, Social Bike Business, specifically supports community leaders who are providing disadvantaged people with affordable, good-quality bicycles designed for transportation as well as job training and jobs. We launched our Social Bike Business program in 2007, our founding year, because we knew from the start that these sorts of programs, once they are underway and sustainable, have a significant, positive impact on bicycling. With eighty percent of the world's population living in or near poverty (World Bank 2008), programs that serve their bicycling needs can reshape whole transportation systems.

In our first year, discussions with community leaders in the U.S., Eastern Europe, and Africa often turned to the lack of affordable, durable transportation bicycles designed for people who live in poverty. To such people, a transportation bicycle can mean the difference between unemployment and a job because bicycling is four to six times faster than walking at common speeds—12 miles per hour for even the least athletic cyclist and two to three miles per hour depending on the age and ability of the walker. A bicycle dramatically extends the distance someone can travel for work without the costs of public transport or a car, either of which can add up to thousands of dollars per year.

The bike industry stopped making quality,

affordable transportation bicycles a long time ago. What we have been left with are bicycles that meet only two of those three criteria—good-quality transportation bikes that cost several months' salary or poor-quality, bicycle-shaped-objects that break down after a few rides, if they are safe to ride at all.

We also hear frequently from partners that even if impoverished people in their communities manage to obtain good-quality transportation bicycles, they have no place to go to get them fixed. Owners of for-profit bike shops focus on selling fancy bicycles to advantaged people in order to meet their monetary bottom line. This means they must locate their stores in upper-class neighborhoods and offer top-of-the-line products. Their staff must be chosen and trained to focus on privileged customers. All of this adds up to a very unwelcoming environment for disadvantaged people and even for some privileged people who want to try bicycling for the first time.

In response, do-it-yourself (DIY), volunteer-run bicycle co-ops and collectives have been popping up in cities across the U.S. and Europe. While the intention is good, their loose organization structures tend to form around the limited time that volunteers can offer. Open hours are often sporadic and unpredictable. Also, many of these programs are based on the do-it-yourself (DIY) concept that only works for people with time to spare. Most disadvantaged people cannot afford the time it takes to build a bike or to learn bicycle repair by trial and error. Much of what these volunteer-run programs set out to accomplish aligns with Social Bike Business. This is why many of our partners for the program started out as volunteer-run operations. Many shifted into more of a social bike business model after the original leaders burned out and they realized that they needed a more sustainable business structure with paid employees.

With for-profit bike shops serving privileged bicycle enthusiasts, and volunteer-run co-ops and collectives serving people with time to spare, most distressed neighborhoods are still left without dependable bike shops that serve the needs of their residents. Anyone who has ever lived on the margins of their society or suffered the stress of poverty knows that impoverished people are not just monetarily poor. Low-paying jobs far from home consume whole days with long work hours and grueling commutes. Childcare and assistance with basic chores are unobtainable luxuries. For those without jobs, social service requirements present an endless maze that crushes the most inspired entrepreneurial spirit. In agricultural areas of the world, simply tending a small plot and caring for animals uses all the energy these food sources provide.

The Social Bike Business program is designed to guide struggling people toward their own entrepreneurial success so they can lift themselves out of poverty. Even obtaining a quality transportation bicycle can save a person several hours each day if they had been walking, and save them thousands of hard-earned dollars each year. Bicycles shrink cities at no charge. The program also helps our partners establish bicycle community centers where struggling people can learn from each other about transportation bicycling and careers in bicycle business and beyond. Our how-to guide for the program, *Defying Poverty with Bicycles: How to Succeed with Your Own Social Bike Business Program*, published in late 2012, covers all the steps needed to launch and manage a sustainable program.

Even as that book was moving toward publication, we were hearing a common cry. Leaders of social bike programs on five continents were desperate for affordable, durable bike parts. Most of these programs rely on donated bicycles, but without suitable parts to repair them, many of these bikes are being set aside. Just as with whole bikes, the bike industry no longer makes basic, good quality yet affordable bike parts. People who ride their bikes daily for transportation and for carrying loads must choose between high-tech racing parts or junk parts made of plastic and pot metal. Both types wear out within a few months of daily use and cannot be repaired.

We realized that a whole new approach was needed to fill this gap. Bike part production had to move back to the local level with simple and affordable designs. Even the production methods had to be redesigned to allow people in the remotest regions and inner cities to make these parts themselves. By creating production methods that anyone can set up in their backyard, we would bypass the markets for inappropriate bike parts, enabling those most in need of durable spare parts to make them themselves and even sell them to others in their region.

As we assessed the possibilities for breaking and reconnecting this chain of bike-part production and sales, a simple casting method stood out as the key. That's why backyard aluminum casting has driven the design of our Bike Shift Lever and will set the stage for future bike parts we take on.

Fortunately, Sue Knaup, our founder and executive director, has a background as a bike shop owner and metal fabricator. When she ran her bike shop in Prescott, Arizona, much of her work involved welding and fabrication of unusual metal projects. Most of the designs for these projects were presented by customers as scribbles on scratch paper. These projects taught Sue that just about anything is possible as long as the goal is clear and you understand the metal you're working with. She still does quite a bit of welding, working with steel, stainless steel, and aluminum. She uses mostly TIG welding, but jumps up to stick welding for big projects. As this project began to point to aluminum casting, Sue engaged her past experience and connected with casting and metal-working colleagues to work out a simple design for shift levers as well as the production method.

Even before Sue sketched the first design of the shift lever, aluminum casting stood out as the clear production method. In fact, scrap aluminum casting drove the final design. We focused on a simple casting method using scrap aluminum that can be collected anywhere in the world. Thus our shift lever can be manufactured by the people who are most affected by the lack of simple, affordable, and repairable shift levers. Once Sue had test melted scrap aluminum in a charcoal furnace built with common items—including a flowerpot furnace body and a steel pipe crucible—our design took shape.

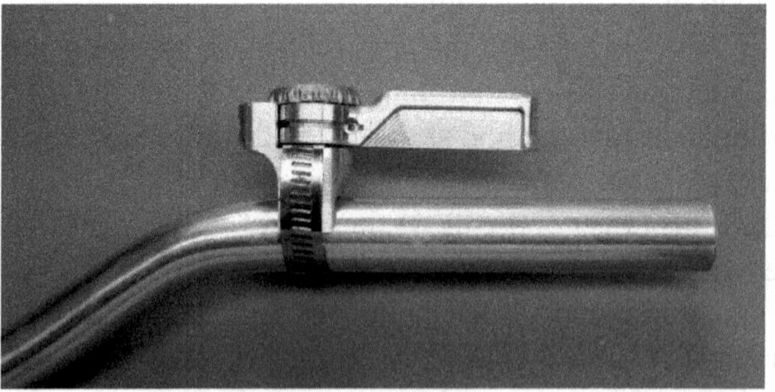

The lever and base of the Bike Shift Lever had to retain simple lines to ensure they could be cast and removed easily from a mold. They also had to be stout enough to hold up to daily use. Sue avoided thin or narrow features that could snap under stress, in a crash, or when the bike was turned upside down for repair. The bolt and cable holes as well as the cable guides proved the most difficult to design, but once these were solved the design fell into place.

As the design took shape, Sue kept our partners and end users in mind. Our shift lever offers several advantages over today's sport-only shift levers:

- Symmetrical—works on right or left side.
- Compatible with all bikes and all gear ranges, front and rear.
- Uses only six parts.
- Easily repaired and customized with common parts.
- Backyard casting using scrap aluminum.
- Simple, durable design for people who depend on their bikes.
- Lever is slightly longer than others and has a broad face for people with weak or injured hands. 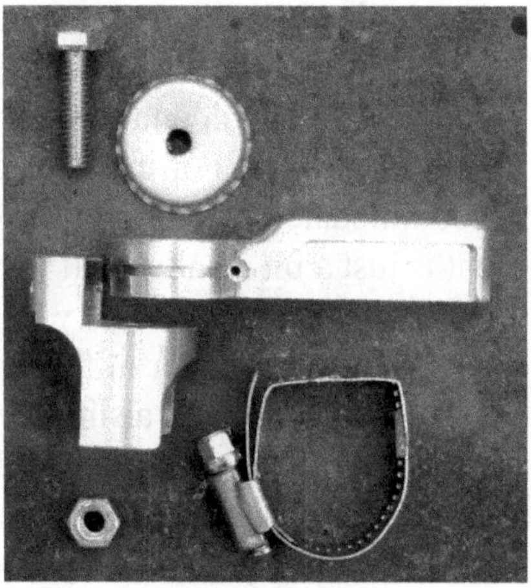
- Supports upside-down bike during repair.
- Uses a hose clamp, a common item found throughout the world.
- Friction is created by spring of stainless steel hose clamp and adjustable bolt tension.
- Bolt and nut are a common size, coarse thread; fits either an 11mm or 7/16" wrench.
- Nut rests inside recessed hex hole in bottom of base so bolt can be tightened easily from the top.

- Bottle cap visually emphasizes DIY design and functions as a slippery washer; customizable.
- Holes in bottle cap and hose clamp can be punched with large nail for easy repair and replacement.

Every element of this design gives priority to durability, affordability, simplicity, and repair. Four of the six parts are common items found in all parts of the world and can easily be replaced by alternate items if necessary. For instance, the hose clamp can be replaced with any similar-sized clamp or, in a remote repair situation, a strap of leather or cloth. While the recommended bolt and nut work best, any bolt and nut combination that are a near match will work. For instance, a longer bolt could be accommodated by adding washers at the top; and a nut that is just a bit smaller will work as long as it can't spin within the hex recess. And while the bottle cap serves as an important reminder of the principles behind this project, it simply functions as a slippery washer. Any thin washer with two smooth surfaces will do the job.

Sue designed the two aluminum parts, the lever and base, so they could be produced by most anyone willing to melt scrap aluminum. Their simple shapes with rounded edges and angles allow smooth flow of the molten aluminum and easy separation from the mold. The two-part steel mold that we will provide to our license partners is compact and easy to handle. Simply connect the two halves, tighten the bolts, and it's ready for the molten aluminum. As soon as the aluminum cools, the caster can open the mold, remove the two parts, reassemble the mold, and pour again. This is the beauty of using a permanent mold.

The design is also ideal for other types of casting, including sand casting and lost wax. While both of those methods are tedious and time consuming, they may work well for readers not interested in becoming one of our license partners in order to receive a permanent mold. There are also methods outside of casting such as CNC machining, 3D printing, and even elegant hand carving using luxurious hardwoods, soft stone, bone, or ceramics. As long as you only want to make a few for your own use, such alternative production methods could be an appealing choice. You'll read more about these and other production alternatives later in this book.

Most importantly, this book will guide you through the steps needed to set up your own foundry and cast these shift levers, or whatever you have in mind. If Bike Shift Levers are your focus, you will learn how to become one of our license partners and receive a permanent casting mold that will hold up to many, many castings. You will also learn about production and finishing methods that will help you increase efficiency and lower costs. Finally, you will find tips on installing and selling these shift levers to further improve your profit margins. These management, pricing, and distribution tips will apply to most any product you'd like to make.

We have a patent pending on the design of our Bike Shift Lever in order to protect the interests of our license partners to sell them at a reasonable price in their particular markets. This licensing information may be noteworthy for you whether you are interested in this shift lever or you plan to develop your own products. You will read more about licensing and use guidelines in the next chapter. While they may seem a diversion from casting, these long-term planning considerations will help you decide your goals for your foundry.

Now let's dig into the licensing guidelines as well as DIY possibilities to help you sort out your own plans for producing Bike Shift Levers or whatever you have in mind.

Chapter 1

License or DIY

Some readers will be interested only in the casting techniques outlined in this book. If you are not interested in making Bike Shift Levers or developing your own business around the products you cast, skip right ahead to Chapter 2 and enjoy the nuances of melting aluminum in a charcoal furnace.

Product development requires a much larger view than simply making a few items for your own use. As you consider your future goals for your casting operation, be sure to account for the potential of expanding into full production. The nice thing about simple backyard casting is that you can start with a small, temporary furnace and then easily expand it. However, many of the decisions you make at the start, including where and how you build your foundry, could save you and your team lots of time, money, and effort if you've kept your long-term goals in mind.

Whether you plan to make Bike Shift Levers or a cast aluminum product of your own design, understanding your production goals will steer important decisions. For instance, if you prefer the low-key, do-it-yourself (DIY) option with a goal of casting only a few items, you have no need for a permanent mold. Then sand casting could be your best choice because you could make many different items with the same foundry setup. You could also stick with a small, less durable furnace structure since you would not need to melt very much aluminum for your limited projects.

However, if you imagine developing a profitable operation around your aluminum casting foundry, you might like to invest in a longer-lasting foundry setup from the start and save yourself the time and frustration of having to rebuild everything once you're underway. If you are interested in producing and selling Bike Shift Levers, a permanent mold will hold up to many, many castings and unlike sand casting, requires little work between pours. Also, a brick furnace will hold up to many more melts than a furnace built with a flowerpot. As you set your plans in place, gauge your level of patience for your particular learning curve as well as your commitment to long-term productivity and profits.

We have invested in the design of the permanent mold for Bike Shift Levers because we look forward to a time when many license partners in remote areas and inner cities of the world will be producing these vital bike parts for their particular regions. Our vision for this project depends on license partners who will provide these shift levers for the people who need them the most. Partners in the remotest areas are topmost to this vision and we cannot expect them to have foundries already set up or even to have electricity available.

The simplest, most durable production method has to be primary, making permanent molds the only option. This is because a permanent mold requires no special training to use. Unlike sand casting and lost wax casting, each of which requires specialized materials and training, a steel permanent mold is as easy to use as an ice tray. Pour in the liquid and let it set.

To make this investment worth our while, we have created strict guidelines for the license partners who will receive a permanent mold. These guidelines accompany our patent pending on our Bike Shift Lever. This will ensure that these expensive molds go only to partners who are serious about producing quality Bike Shift Levers for a long time. With these license agreements for mold recipients, we will also have a means to ensure that each of our partners is truly committed to helping people with bikes. The people we license with will hold a leadership role in an established organization that is incorporated as a nonprofit, nongovernmental organization (NGO), or social enterprise with a purpose focused on beneficial bicycle programs.

Even though we have a patent pending on our Bike Shift Lever, we also want this project to inspire innovators to design all sorts of simple, durable bike parts that anyone can repair and even make themselves. The DIY and maker movements are near and dear to our hearts because this fertile ground is where alternatives to the race-fixated bike industry will sprout.

As you consider your own plans for your backyard aluminum casting foundry, let your creativity flow to other parts of bicycles that may need simpler designs. We're doing the same with One Street Components, looking ahead to the next bike part we should tackle. Talk to people in your area to find out which bike parts they are having trouble finding and which ones no longer hold up to daily use. Try developing these bike products. Or, if you're happy sticking with Bike Shift Levers or your own project, drop us a line with your ideas for the next bike part we should take on.

Our patent protection for our Bike Shift Lever will give us control over the quality and sales distribution of this particular product. This also ensures that potential license partners interested in producing them to high quality standards will know these protections are in place for their sales market. They won't have to worry that another manufacturer will flood the market with underpriced (even free) or inferior shift levers that would undercut their ability to sustain their business of making and selling these shift levers.

The choice whether to license with us or not should be easy. You simply have to decide whether you only want to make a few Bike Shift Levers for your own use or whether you plan to sell them. There will be unique situations where the decision remains unclear. To help distinguish the two options, a license partner expects to produce and sell Bike Shift Levers as they are designed. A license partner also has to be an established nonprofit organization with bicycle programs. In contrast, a do-it-yourself (DIY) person only plans to produce a few shift levers and perhaps experiment with the design and production method, but cannot sell the shifters or give them away. A license partner can certainly experiment, but not with the Bike Shift Levers they sell.

The list below outlines the license restrictions in more detail and will be part of our license agreement with each of our partners. While these restrictions help guide our license agreement, they also apply to anyone, licensed or not. Each restriction is designed to help our partners focus their efforts toward producing high-quality shifters and at the same time, assure them that others cannot undermine their good work. These restrictions should also help clarify the options that you and your team have before you.

LICENSE RESTRICTIONS:

- Bike Shift Levers cannot be sold at all—whether separately, as part of a package, as part of a bicycle, or in any other way—without an approved license agreement with One Street Components covering the calendar year of the sale.
- Bike Shift Levers cannot be given away unless attached and functioning as a shift lever on a bicycle, whether a license is in place or not. Once such giveaways reach a total of ten, no matter the time period, a license agreement will have to be set in place in order to continue.
- Bike Shift Levers have to be sold at a price that supports the manufacturer's business and is comparable to the price of Bike Shift Levers being sold in nearby markets. This includes online sales.
- Any infringement of any patents on the Bike Shift Lever is strictly forbidden.
- Any modification to the design of the Bike Shift Levers produced under the license will void and sever a license agreement.

That should help you imagine your potential for producing these shift levers. A license partner will also receive from us significant benefits in the form of assistance, promotion, and endorsement of your product quality. We will also help license partners develop their sales plans, find bulk suppliers of parts and materials, and connect with distributors that serve retailers in their area.

Next are details regarding the license agreement option. After that you will find details on the DIY option. Take the time to compare these options with what you and your team have in mind before you decide on the one that fits your plans the best.

LICENSE AGREEMENT

License partners have to be an incorporated nonprofit NGO or social enterprise with a purpose that prioritizes helping people with bicycles. First they will need to agree to the above restrictions and then will buy-in at a one-time, non-negotiable fee. This fee covers the cost of the mold and jig, plus the administration required to establish them as a license partner. It does not include shipping or import taxes that might apply. Even if a license partner believes they will not need a particular item in the buy-in package, the buy-in fee remains the same for all license partners each calendar year. This buy-in fee will be determined at the start of each year for new license partners and will only increase in later years if the associated costs increase.

Annual renewal for license partners will require inspection of a Bike Shift Lever produced within the same month of the renewal application, plus a small renewal fee. This renewal fee will help to offset One Street's administration costs and support our efforts to promote our license partners.

Find the latest buy-in price for new Bike Shift Lever license partners along with renewal fees on the One Street Components web page under Programs at www.onestreet.org.

Once approved, each license partner will receive a buy-in package for producing Bike Shift Levers that includes:

- One permanent casting mold for casting both the lever and the base.
- One jig for finishing the parts and instructions for using it.
- One sample shift lever.
- One copy of this book.

- A personalized badge in digital format authorizing the partner to produce Bike Shift Levers for that calendar year to be used in packaging and marketing materials. Badges for future years will be issued after a sample shift lever from that year's production is sent to One Street Components for inspection and approval and the annual renewal fee is paid.
- Assistance finding bulk supplies including parts for the Bike Shift Lever as well as packaging art and materials.
- Assistance connecting with distributors and creating promotions in the partner's particular region.
- Listing as an authorized One Street Components Bike Shift Lever manufacturer on the One Street website for each year the license is in effect.

License partners will also be authorized to purchase extra molds and jigs from us as well as participate in our bulk parts orders.

Ongoing support will also be available from One Street for license partners who encounter issues during production. For instance, if your furnace does not melt your scrap aluminum properly or you find that some scraps are behaving strangely before they melt, you could simply call or email for tips and ideas. Even beyond the foundry operations, you can call or email us for ideas on pricing, sales, and marketing your Bike Shift Levers to people in your unique community.

This on-call support aligns with One Street's mission to serve any leader of any bicycle organization. Innovators who are looking to move beyond this product to help more people ride bicycles are welcome to contact us for basic assistance. Backyard aluminum casting has become a highlight of our work as it opens so many new doors for local bike part production no matter where someone lives in the world. We are happy to help anyone who is also engaged in developing simple yet effective production methods in order to bring the production of bike parts, and even whole bicycles, back to the communities where they will be bought and used. While our license partners will receive much more intensive assistance, we can at least offer you some ideas on your product development and perhaps connect you with useful resources.

Furthermore, approved license partners can request a visit from a One Street Components trainer to assist in the setup of their foundry and the training of their employees. While this book covers the usual steps needed to start and begin using a backyard aluminum casting foundry, your situation could have some unique issues to overcome. For instance, you might have a fantastic building available for your manufacturing operation, but your outdoor area is limited, requiring a special design for your furnace. You might also like to connect with one of our trainers to train not only you and your fellow leaders in foundry setup, but train your employees in safe and efficient aluminum casting.

A visit from one of us could be worth the time and expense to ensure that your setup is the best it can be and that it is what you will need for your long-term plans. Such a visit would come with additional travel and accommodation costs for the trainer, but we are happy to assist with the fundraising needed to cover those costs.

A more affordable and, in the long term, more valuable option is to work with experts in your area. While One Street can offer general advice and guidance on program setup and casting, there is no substitute for developing good relationships with your local metalworkers and business owners to help you set up your operation.

As you consider the potential of becoming a license partner to manufacture Bike Shift Levers you will want to assess the various costs involved and compare them to your likely sales of these shifters. In later chapters you will learn about setting up your foundry and creating an efficient production line along with the shop setup, tools, and number of people you will need. The job of producing these shift levers can be done by one person or be split into specific tasks. For instance, it could be done with four employees:

1) preparing and melting the scrap aluminum,
2) pouring and tending the mold,
3) finishing and
4) assembly.

This four-employee setup would allow each person to focus on their particular element of the operation and help ensure that each pays attention to their particular safety needs. It would also release one or two of them to prepare more scrap aluminum for melting between pours.

Another option would have two employees:

1) preparing, melting, and pouring,
2) finishing and assembly.

While a two-employee operation is not as efficient as four, it still allows greater focus and efficiency than if the entire operation has to be done by one. With two employees, you could also look at staggering these operations per day with both employees working the furnace one day, then both finishing and assembling the shifters the next.

Efficiency will increase with more workers, but so will the costs, so you will need to test and track your results in order to find the right mix that ensures a sustainable profit. Purchasing multiple molds will also increase efficiency as they can be lined up for quick pouring of several shift levers at once. An extra jig or two for finishing the parts could also increase production output. You can find current prices for extra molds and jigs on the One Street Components web page noted earlier in this chapter.

DO-IT-YOURSELF (DIY)

The DIY option is straightforward because you simply need to follow the restrictions listed earlier in this chapter. As long as you only make a few shift levers for your own use, you will not be infringing on any issued patent that results from or relates to our pending patent or accompanying restrictions. However, if you find yourself wanting to make ten or more Bike Shift Levers for your friends and family, no matter the time period, know that you will be at that infringement line. Before you move into production, contact us to discuss a license agreement.

Also note that production method is not part of our pending patent. Whether you cast the parts, chisel them, or create them on a CNC machine, all of the restrictions noted earlier in this chapter apply.

Now let's move on to the fun of setting up your foundry, sorting out scrap aluminum, and watching it melt into that lovely silver liquid.

Chapter 2

Foundry and Casting Basics

A fully equipped foundry for casting aluminum can be set up on a tight budget as long as the location and workforce are ready to go. This chapter starts with the list of items needed to succeed. From this basic setup you and your team can shift and expand the various foundry elements to meet the needs of your particular casting operation. So, look especially at the principles behind each element, for instance the use of fired clay for the furnace body.

Fired clay works well for the furnace body because it was fired at high temperatures in a kiln and thus it holds up to high temperatures. There are many vessels and bricks made out of this material. The list suggests starting with a flowerpot because that is a very common item, but any fired-clay container, or bricks made of fired clay, would work. Any container made of a non-toxic metal such as steel or iron would also work because the furnace body simply needs to contain the charcoal. Metal, however, will pull more heat away than fired clay and thus reduce the efficiency of your furnace. Near the end of this chapter, under Furnace Care and Alternatives, you'll read about expanding your furnace using fired clay bricks. The size and materials of each foundry element you choose should follow the principles of its function as well as your casting goals and budget.

As you and your team prepare to manufacture Bike Shift Levers, or any other product expected to be profitable, you will want to assess what resources are available and needed in order to reach what you see as full production. Even a hobbyist needs to know these details in order to budget accordingly. Consider not only the place for your foundry, but the funding and supplies you have or can acquire. Use the following list of supplies and resources to create a budget with prices in your area. This time will be well spent because you do not want to get halfway into your project and have to stop for lack of funds or supplies.

Set up your budget with realistic funding sources at the top. Note whether they are currently available. Otherwise, note a target date when you expect to receive the funds so that you can plan accordingly. Below the income section start your expenses section where you will list all your expected costs for your initial production run. Include not only supplies, but employee wages, rent, transportation of supplies, and overhead costs such as computer, phone, and office supplies. Assessing all of these costs at the beginning will not only help you succeed with start up, but will become the basis for your pricing system to ensure profitability once you're up and running. The following list only includes likely items that most readers will need. Be sure to consider and include all of the expenses that your particular project will encounter.

LIST OF SUPPLIES AND RESOURCES

- **Dry outdoor dirt area:** with at least 20 feet (six meters) cleared radius all around the furnace, no concrete (the moisture held in concrete explodes on contact with molten aluminum) or combustibles within this area. In wet regions you may need a high roof, but leave off walls to ensure proper ventilation.

Keep molten aluminum away from concrete.

- **Employee wages:** casting is hard work, so hiring more people will help ease the load; one to tend the furnace with others pouring and assembling will work best.
- **Scrap aluminum:** find reliable sources in your area; consider transportation, storage, and sometimes purchase costs.
- **Magnet:** to distinguish steel from aluminum.
- **Bike Shift Lever mold:** consider purchasing more than one to increase production; for other products, work with a local mold maker or learn sand-casting mold methods.
- **Bike Shift Lever parts:** calculate number needed for first production run; bolts, nuts, hose clamps, and bottle caps. Use a sample Bike Shift Lever to spec parts available in your area.
- **Bike Shift Lever parts jig:** will guide your drill for finishing holes in cast parts and assist with punching holes in the bottle caps and clamps.
- **Steel punch or nail with flat end:** for removing core pin from lever.
- **Steel punch or nail with sharp end:** for punching holes in caps and clamps.
- **Hammer:** for preparing scrap aluminum, releasing parts from mold and core pin, and punching holes.
- **Chisel or hatchet:** for opening mold.

- **Drill and bits:** a hand drill will work, though an electric drill press is ideal; 1/16" (2mm) bit for cable holes, 1/4" (6mm) bit for housing holes.
- **Hacksaw or electric band saw:** to cut extra aluminum off parts from sprues and vents.
- **Hand files (also electric sander if possible):** to remove extra aluminum at saw cut and seam, and clean holes.
- **Wrenches/spanners for assemblers:** 7/16" or 11mm
- **Flowerpot, other fired clay vessel, or fired clay bricks to build with**: use fired clay only (fired at high temperature in a kiln), not adobe or concrete; use as furnace body, approximately ten inch (25cm) diameter and eight inches (20cm) tall to fit into a hole dug just larger than it; dry sand to fill space between hole and furnace for insulation.
- **Steel pipe:** at least one foot long (30cm), bent to fit bottom of furnace and attached to air supply hose on the other end. Diameter depends on your furnace design and air supply, but one inch (2.5cm) is plenty. Wall thickness can be as thin as 1/32 inch (1mm) since it will not have to withstand much heat.
- **Hose:** to connect steel pipe to air supply.
- **Air supply:** to attach to hose; any hand pump, foot pump, or bellows will work. If cheap electricity is available, a small blower such as a hair

dryer set on cool will work.

- **Lid:** to cover furnace; a steel or iron pan or something made from fired clay works well.
- **Charcoal:** look for suppliers of bulk charcoal in your area.
- **Separate fire pit:** can be a BBQ or other device for starting charcoal, preheating crucible, breaking cast aluminum, and drying cans.
- **Crucible:** where aluminum will melt, made of steel; can be a piece of three- to four-inch-diameter pipe (7.5cm to 10cm) with a wall thickness of about 1/8 inch (3mm), about six inches (15cm) long plugged on one end and a long handle welded on. A steel or iron pot of similar dimensions will work as well.
- **Tongs:** made of steel, for adding scrap to crucible.
- **Vise:** four-inch (10mm) minimum to hold parts for finishing; also handy for preparing metal.
- **Work bench:** best welded out of steel; to hold vise and a few furnace tools.
- **Slag spoon:** for stirring molten metal and removing slag; any small spoon made of steel or stainless steel; may need to weld on a longer handle.
- **Cupcake or biscuit pans:** these are ideal for pouring extra aluminum to create good-sized ingots as well as for dumping slag.
- **Safety gear:** for everyone working around the furnace:
    - eye protection,
    - heavy leather gloves,
    - full covering of natural-fiber clothes such as cotton, wool, or leather (no

synthetics—they are flammable!) including shoes, socks, pants/skirt, long sleeves, and hat. Pants and shirts should not be rolled up or have cuffs where hot splatters could be caught.

No synthetic clothing.

- **Pile of dry sand, shovel, and water supply nearby:** to extinguish fires. Warning! Do not allow water near molten aluminum as it will explode as soon as it touches the molten aluminum! Use sand to extinguish fires near the furnace. Use water only if the fire spreads away from the furnace.

Keep water away from molten aluminum!

SETTING UP YOUR FOUNDRY

Once you have collected and established everything on this list and read through the next chapter, you should be ready to melt some scrap aluminum. Plan to run several test melts, pouring only into your cupcake pans to create ingots as you learn and fine tune your furnace. You can re-melt these ingots later when you are ready to use your mold. Write ample notes on how your particular furnace functions, to use for employee training later on.

You will note a few warnings in the list of supplies regarding keeping moisture away from molten aluminum. This is extremely important as any moisture that comes into contact with it will flash boil, blasting molten aluminum onto your workers. Keeping liquids away should be easy to explain and enforce, but also keep in mind that anything that holds moisture also holds this danger. This is why you need to keep the molten aluminum away from concrete. Concrete slabs, sidewalks, and even concrete blocks used for building all hold moisture. Even a drop of molten aluminum onto concrete can explode. Also, if you plan to melt aluminum drink cans, be sure they are completely dry before placing them into your crucible. Lay them next to a fire or out in the sun to speed the drying process.

Dry drink cans before melting.

This is why a dry dirt area is ideal for your furnace. If it rains frequently enough to keep this area moist, you may need to build a roof over your foundry to keep the ground dry wherever molten aluminum will be present. In case your area has a particular and severe rainy season, consider planning ahead to cast an ample supply of shifters when it is dry. Then spend the rainy season finishing, assembling, and selling your shift levers. A similar scheduling plan might work well in areas with harsh winters or summers when working outside would be miserable.

Ensure proper ventilation by leaving walls off.

If you decide you need a roof over your furnace, leave off walls to ensure proper ventilation. Scrap aluminum often has toxic paints and colors added. As these burn in your furnace, you want your workers to avoid breathing the smoke it emits, at least until these toxins have burned off. Also, when charcoal burns it creates carbon monoxide, which has no smell and can be deadly if too much is inhaled, so never burn charcoal inside an enclosure. While some homes are set up to burn charcoal safely with proper ventilation, a charcoal furnace emits far more carbon monoxide than a home fire and thus requires much greater ventilation.

Aluminum itself is not toxic to most people because it passes right through us. As the most prevalent metal in the earth's crust, we consume it normally in our food and water without any problem. It's also a common ingredient in antacids, antiperspirants, sunscreen, and other products we ingest and apply to our skin because of its beneficial effects and easy elimination by the body. The only exposure you and your workers will have around your foundry will be from touching the aluminum and possibly ingesting or breathing aluminum dust. Since aluminum doesn't vaporize until reaching its boiling point over 4,000°F (2,300°C), you won't have to worry about aluminum fumes from your furnace. But even if you did, aluminum fumes behave the same—they simply pass out of us without being absorbed. But as with anything, it is possible to be exposed to too much. People with kidney disease are far more susceptible to overexposure to toxins, even aluminum, so they should not work around your foundry.

Symptoms of overexposure to toxins include confusion, weakness, and speech problems. Watch your workers and train them to watch each other. If anyone exhibits such symptoms move them away from the furnace immediately. If they don't recover right away, seek medical attention.

Watch for symptoms of overexposure to toxins.

As you plan the design of your foundry, also keep in mind the best materials to use. Fired clay bricks do not carry the same danger as concrete because fired clay does not hold moisture as long as concrete does, though you still need to ensure that it is dry. This is why a flowerpot, other fired clay vessel, or fired clay bricks work as the main furnace body. Consider laying out dry fired clay bricks to create a solid platform where workers can stand as well as clean places to set tools and keep things organized.

Steel is the other material you will see repeated throughout the supply list. This is because steel melts at twice the temperature of aluminum: 1,200°F (660°C) compared to 2,600°F (1,450°C) for steel. Even the Bike Shift Lever mold is made out of steel. Your steel crucible should withstand many pours, as should the steel pipe you insert into the bottom of your furnace. This section of pipe should be at least one foot (30cm) long to allow you to attach a plastic pump or blower hose to it without the plastic melting. This section of pipe can be quite thin-walled, even as thin as 1/32 inch (1mm), as long as it is steel. The larger diameter piece of pipe you use for your crucible and the flat piece you weld on as the bottom should each be about 1/8 inch (3mm) thick. Any thinner and it won't hold up to as many pours. Any thicker and it won't heat enough to melt your aluminum properly.

Dig your furnace hole just larger than your pot or brick assembly to allow you to pack dry sand all around it. This sand layer will act as insulation, but doesn't need to be more than a few inches thick. The job of your clay pot or bricks is to hold the charcoal. Some backyard casters simply dig a hole and fill it with charcoal, but this is wasteful because charcoal at the edge of the hole will lose heat to the soil. With a clay pot or brick furnace just large enough to set coals all around your crucible, you will save significant amounts of charcoal and thus time and money. This all contributes to a profitable casting enterprise. Also, even the driest soil will tend to hold some moisture. While it may not be enough to cause a flash boil, even a bit of moisture will draw heat away from your furnace. Containing your coals in a clay pot or brick structure and packing dry sand all around it will insulate the coals from the moist, cool soil.

Place in the bottom of your hole a few rocks or fired-clay bricks for your pot to sit on leaving a gap to accommodate the bent end of the steel pipe. If using bricks, a steel plate laid on one layer of bricks works well. Drill or cut a hole in the middle of this plate and weld or otherwise attach your steel air-supply pipe to the bottom. The end of the pipe should insert as little as possible into the pot or plate to allow the air that it pumps in to flow to even the lowest pieces of charcoal. From the furnace, dig a narrow trench for the pipe and hose to lie easily. When you pack the sand around the furnace, and after the pipe and hose are situated as you want them, you can also fill in this trench. This will remove this possible trip hazard.

Make sure the hose extends well past the hole, approximately six feet (two meters), so your workers can avoid the furnace fumes if they are using a hand or foot pump. If you can use an electrical or other mechanical pump, a shorter hose is fine. Match this hose to your chosen pump or create a way to connect them without air loss. Before filling in the trench for the hose, test the amount of air your pump generates through the hole in the furnace. It must be enough to turn the coals red hot. It also needs to operate for several hours to keep them that way, depending on your pouring schedule.

Consider the way your pump is used and the comfort of the workers who will have to keep pumping it. If you can use an electrical pump, a small vacuum cleaner set on blow or a good-quality hair dryer (set on cool to prevent it burning out) will provide ample air and should hold up for long stretches of melting. Avoid high-powered blowers. Too much air will create too much heat, wasting charcoal, ruining your crucible, and overheating your aluminum.

When using a flowerpot as your furnace body, you will need to make a notch in its rim to accommodate the handle of your crucible and to allow smoke and fumes to escape. You want your lid to fit well in order to retain heat, so creating a notch is important for venting, even when using bricks. With a flowerpot or other fired-clay vessel, it's easy to make such a notch using a pair of pliers by gently nibbling away at the rim until you achieve a notch just larger than your crucible's handle.

Set up your work area around your furnace so that everything you will need is in reach, but will not cause a trip hazard. Make sure the area is level and has no unnecessary debris. This will allow you or one of your workers to lift the crucible from the furnace and pour into the mold without having to make unnecessary movements while handling this dangerous molten metal.

FURNACE CARE and ALTERNATIVES

Always cover your furnace to prevent rain, sun, and wind damage. After each day of casting, clean out all of the old ash and charcoal to ensure your pipe is still connected and not filled in with ash. After cleaning out all the ash, work your pump to blow any remaining ash out of the pipe.

If you choose to use a flowerpot for your furnace body, know that it will crack early on. This is normal and will not be a problem as long as it holds its shape since its only job is to contain the charcoal. Most flowerpots will eventually crack enough that they have to be replaced, perhaps after four or five long casting days. Taking time to cover and protect your furnace will ensure that it lasts as long as possible. Have some spare pots on hand for quick replacement when needed.

Once you are underway and producing acceptable Bike Shift Levers or other items, you may want to expand your furnace and make it last longer to increase efficiency.

One easy way is to upgrade it to a fired-brick furnace. Dig a larger hole and line it with fired bricks to create a furnace hole about the same size as the one provided by your old flowerpot. Because you can't use mortar, you will need to find or make a bottom plate of either fired clay or steel. This plate will need to withstand extreme heat from the charcoal and it will need a hole in its center (much like the flowerpot hole) for your air supply. If you choose a steel plate, welding the pipe to the underside at this hole will make for a long-lasting base for your furnace. Lay the plate on top of a layer of bricks at the bottom of your hole. The brick layer needs to leave just enough space for the air pipe. Alternatively, you can shift your air supply to the side through the bricks, but then you will have to run your steel pipe through to the other side of the furnace with holes all along it (or at least at the center of the furnace) to ensure that the air reaches all coals as evenly as possible.

This book has provided the steps you need for a basic furnace that will serve many fine melts, but increasing production might eventually be of interest to you. Lots of clever designs are posted on the internet with larger charcoal beds, crucibles that require two people to lift, gas burners, massive blowers, and other elements. Do a search for "how to build a smelting furnace" for countless ideas. You will even find some that are made to be mobile.

Now that you have everything you need to set up your own aluminum casting foundry, we can move on to the next chapter where we'll explore the intricacies of scrap aluminum and melting it down into that silvery liquid.

Chapter 3

Working with and Melting Scrap Aluminum

Not only is aluminum the most abundant metal in the earth's crust, it is one of the most common materials used to make just about every type of product. Depending on the number of people who earn their living collecting scrap metal in your area, you might have a very easy or rather tough time finding it. This chapter will delve into how to recognize scrap aluminum and offer tips for creating an ongoing supply so you never have to worry about running out.

Later in the chapter we'll look at the finer details involved in melting scrap aluminum to ensure that your castings are high quality.

WORKING WITH SCRAP ALUMINUM

Scrap aluminum is surprisingly easy to find in all areas of the world. Once you set your sights on finding it, you will discover it in the form of drink cans, cooking pots, engine parts, lawn chair frames, gutters, window frames, posts, signs, bike parts; the list is long. Carry a magnet with you so you can distinguish steel, which sticks to a magnet, from aluminum, which does not. Even using a magnet, you might still be fooled by stainless steel because, depending on its particular alloys, stainless steel may not stick to a magnet. But just as with any steel, stainless steel is about three times heavier than aluminum and it won't melt in your furnace so you will soon learn the difference. Another way to distinguish aluminum from steel, including stainless steel, is that aluminum does not make sparks when touched by an electric grinder. But steel will always send out a shower of sparks.

Zinc is another metal that is easily confused with aluminum, especially cast zinc. It has a similar look and also does not stick to a magnet. However, like steel it is about three times heavier than aluminum. Find something that you are sure is aluminum and is of a similar size and compare their weights. If the item in question is zinc, its heavier weight will be obvious. Also, pour a small puddle of vinegar onto the metal. If it is zinc the vinegar will fizz and bubble. If it is aluminum nothing will happen. You'll find a table of aluminum alloys and their common uses in Appendix A. While you'll see that the 7xxx series aluminum is alloyed with zinc, the zinc comprises less than six percent of the resultant metal and so has only a small influence over how it behaves when melted.

Zinc's similarity to steel ends at weight. It melts at just under 800°F (427°C) which is well below aluminum's melting point of about 1,200°F (660°C). This makes zinc a popular metal for casting low-cost metal items such as household fixtures and even accessory car parts. Recall that steel melts 2,600°F (1,450°C) so if a stray piece ends up in your crucible it is easy to note your mistake and simply remove the unmelted steel chunk. But a stray chunk of zinc will not be as easy to detect.

The main concern about melting zinc is that its fumes are toxic. When zinc is simply melting this is not a

Zinc fumes are toxic.

problem because it is not yet emitting fumes. But zinc vaporizes at about 1,600°F (871°C), a temperature that would be easy to reach with your backyard furnace. Because cast zinc is heavier than aluminum, the resultant parts would feel and behave differently from your aluminum cast parts. Zinc is a common metal used in pot metal, which is a mix of cheap, low-melting-point metals used for toys and other low-cost metal items. Pot metal is known for its low strength and brittleness. While zinc adds strength to certain aluminum alloys, these alloys depend on exact proportions and proper handling of the zinc. We do not recommend messing with zinc, mainly because your workers would be exposed to its toxic fumes. Besides that danger, zinc would cause a noticeable difference in your castings, including increased weight and potential weakening of the resultant part.

Magnesium burns explosively.

You will also need to learn the difference between cast aluminum and cast magnesium, which is more difficult to determine. Magnesium is only slightly lighter, looks quite similar to cast aluminum, and melts at a similar temperature. Magnesium is dangerous to melt because it catches fire explosively. Train your workers to look out for it and pull it from your scrap piles. Fortunately, magnesium is at least fifty percent more expensive than aluminum so magnesium products are rarer. Most are cast, though extruded magnesium products are occasionally made. Common uses of cast magnesium include airplane parts, some "mag" wheels for cars (though most are actually aluminum), chainsaw motors, and Volkswagen engine parts. If you find a piece of scrap that may be magnesium, you can perform two simple tests:

1. As with the zinc test, pour a small puddle of cheap vinegar (for instance white or cider vinegar) onto the metal. If it is magnesium, the vinegar will fizz and make bubbles. If it is aluminum, there will be no reaction.
2. Use a file to shave off a small pile of shavings from the piece. Set this pile away from the questionable metal and other potential flammables. Light a match and hold it to the shavings. If it is magnesium, these shavings will burst into flame after a short time. If it is aluminum they will not catch fire.

As you can see in the Table of Aluminum Alloys in Appendix A, both zinc and magnesium are common alloying elements for aluminum, but only in small quantities. For instance, as already noted, zinc is the major alloying element in the 7xxx series aluminum adding strength and improving heat treatment and machining results, but making it more difficult to weld. Magnesium is a major alloying element in the 5xxx and 6xxx series aluminum alloys, improving machinability. Since the amounts of zinc and magnesium are so small in these aluminum alloys you do not have to worry about zinc fumes or magnesium burning when melting them.

Tin is another metal you might worry about, but it should not cause any problems. Tin is a very soft metal that melts at 450ºF (232ºC). It is rarely used in its pure form except in decorative pieces because it is so soft. Most tin in the world is used in solder. Other applications are as plating of steel cans (this is why they are often called "tin cans") and as an alloy in bronze and brass. You will easily detect tin-plated steel cans with your magnet. Bronze and brass have a yellow color that set them apart from aluminum.

Carefully train all your workers to look out for steel, zinc, and magnesium as they sort and prepare your scrap aluminum. Teach them about the dangers of zinc and magnesium to underscore the necessity to test every piece of scrap they are not sure is aluminum. And remind them to keep all moisture away from the molten aluminum at all times, including the hidden liquid that is commonly left in drink cans.

Use the Table of Aluminum Alloys in Appendix A to sort the scraps you collect. Create at least three categories to help you determine which type you are melting. Drink cans and sheet metal should go together. All cast aluminum should go into a separate pile or bin. Bike parts can be placed with structural aluminum pieces. More about this as we delve into melting aluminum.

One of the easiest ways to collect scrap aluminum is to put out the call to your friends, relatives, and community. When they learn about your Bike Shift Lever project (or other projects) many will be happy to help by getting rid of broken aluminum items and drink cans they've accumulated. Place collection bins where people can easily deliver their scrap.

Reach out to construction companies, auto repair shops, bike shops, and secondhand stores and ask if they could collect aluminum for you. Even your local scrap dealers may sell you scrap aluminum at a discount in order to help the project. You may know people who make their living collecting and selling recyclables to the dealers. They may be happy to sell you aluminum at a similar price they get from the dealers, which will likely be far lower than the dealers' price. Go to flea markets and yard sales on the last day when sellers are often eager to sell their aluminum items at a low price to get rid of them.

Most of the aluminum you collect will need to be

cut, broken or reshaped in order to fit into your crucible. Melting thin pieces can waste aluminum and fuel because the more surface area exposed to air during the melt, the more oxygen will attach to the aluminum turning it into slag that must be removed. Crush drink cans top to bottom and, if needed, smash them again with a hammer to reduce surface area as much as possible. Hammer thin strips of aluminum into tight chunks.

Cast aluminum pieces are often too large to fit into your crucible, but they are surprisingly easy to break into small pieces. Unlike steel, aluminum becomes brittle just before it melts. Place a large cast piece into a fire pit or BBQ on top of hot coals then cover it with more coals and perhaps a lid to retain the heat. When it is ready to be struck, it will either appear to sweat or it will drop early melt drops from its edges. At this stage, all you need to do is remove it with tongs or long pliers, place it on a hard surface, and hit it with a hammer to make it crumble into small bits. Do this quickly as it will cool back to the non-brittle state almost immediately. You'll find that with a large piece you will likely have to place it back into the fire a few times before you are able to break all of it into small pieces this way.

You can also use such a fire to soften long strips of aluminum for smashing and bending to fit into your crucible. This fire will do a good job of burning off most of the paint and color coatings. Placing it at some distance from where most of your workers are working will disperse these potentially harmful fumes before the metal goes into your furnace. Set drink cans near this fire to dry out any remaining liquid before melting, but not so close that they oxidize. You can see them oxidize when they turn a darker color.

In dry climates, drink cans can be dried simply by

waiting a week or more before melting them. Placing them in the sun will speed the drying even more. If you have the time, drying your cans this way will avoid the potential of oxidizing them in your fire. But a fire is a good option for wet climates and for quick-turnaround situations where wet cans must be melted immediately.

If you have an electric chop saw or other sort of saw that you can use with a strong clamp, this is a good way to cut long strips into pieces small enough for your crucible. Stipulate that anyone using such an electric saw must wear safety glasses and ear protection. They should also know how to safely use the saw, including only cutting pieces that can be clamped or laid against the saw's fence. Even the best saw will tend to fling metal shards into the person using it, so eye protection is a must. Shoes, long pants (or skirt), and long sleeves are also a good idea. When a high-speed saw blade cuts metal it makes a tremendous, high-pitched noise that will damage ears, so ear protection should also be required.

Never use an abrasive cutting blade or grinding wheel on aluminum.

Never use an abrasive metal cutting blade to cut aluminum with an electric saw. Abrasive metal cutting blades are made for ferrous metals, that is, steel and iron. They have no teeth and look more like a cutting wheel than a saw blade. They slice through steel by generating heat at the cut, but as soon as they hit aluminum their pores fill with the soft metal, causing heat to build up until they explode. So stick with toothed saw blades with carbide tips. For instance, a ten-inch-diameter (25cm) blade with 48 total teeth or more will work well on thin aluminum. If you must use a blade with fewer teeth, just go slowly to allow the teeth to cut rather than catch on the metal.

The same concern applies for electric grinding wheels or cutting wheels used with a grinder. Later in the book we'll look at tools for finishing your parts. If you would like an electrical finishing option, a band saw is a good choice for cutting extra aluminum from your parts and a belt sander works well for smoothing rough edges.

As you sort, cut, and smash your scrap, remove all non-aluminum pieces. While plastics, paper, and such will burn off in your furnace, they will also introduce impurities. It's impossible to prevent all impurities and most will be captured as slag that floats to the top to be removed, but keeping them to a minimum will improve the quality of the molten aluminum you produce.

MELTING ALUMINUM

Depending on the energy source you use for your air supply, you may want to start your charcoal in the separate fire pit since it won't need pumped air. You and your workers will especially appreciate this if you are using a hand pump as your furnace's air supply. As the charcoal is getting hot, place your crucible next to these coals to preheat it. Do the same with any cans you suspect to still contain liquid so they will dry completely. If there's room, place the other pieces of scrap you're planning to melt next to this fire. This will preheat them so they won't cool the molten aluminum as much as cold pieces do.

Once the coals are starting to ash on the edges, place a double layer of them in the bottom of your furnace, then place your pre-heated crucible on top of them. Fill the rest of the furnace with charcoal so your crucible is completely surrounded and start your pump or blower.

The first aluminum you place in the crucible should be thick pieces, even a quarter inch thick or more if you have some. Thick aluminum is generally produced either by extrusion, forging, or casting. Reference the table in Appendix A to get an idea of the sorts of thick pieces you might find in your area. Thick pieces will have less surface area to oxidize and so will reach the melting point without creating much slag, which is generally comprised of oxidized aluminum. Even if you are short on pieces that are as thick or thicker than a quarter inch, anything with some thickness will be better than trying to start your pool with drink cans or similarly thin material as they oxidize just before melting. One of aluminum's most distinguishing characteristics is that it readily bonds to oxygen and this bond causes oxidation.

In fact, even though aluminum is the most abundant metal in the earth's crust, it was the most precious metal in the world through most of the 1800s. This was because no one could figure out how to extract it from oxygen as well as the other elements it likes to adhere to. Once Charles Hall figured it out in 1886 using a particular chemical solution and electrolysis process, aluminum prices plummeted. Other inventors around the world also discovered and engaged the process further driving the price down. This was no problem for Mr. Hall as he had founded the company that eventually became Aluminum Company of America (Alcoa) within two years of his great discovery and had cornered the market.

Aluminum retains its endearing attraction to oxygen even after extraction, which is one of its beneficial characteristics. New aluminum parts quickly oxidize on their surface. This oxidized aluminum is many times harder than pure aluminum and prevents harmful oxidation and other corrosions suffered by other metals such as rust on steel. However, this oxidation presents a problem when melting aluminum because any surface that is allowed to oxidize just prior to melting will turn into this harder aluminum oxide and become slag that must be discarded. A bit of slag acts as a protective coating at the top of the melt, but beyond that, it is only waste material.

The surface area of drink cans and other thin-walled items is so great, even after they are smashed, oxygen finds vast areas on which to attach itself, turning much of the aluminum to dusty slag instead of melting. By creating a nice pool of molten aluminum from thick pieces before adding your first can, you will make it possible to submerge these thin-walled pieces before losing them to oxidation.

Even after melting thick pieces, you will notice a layer of slag at the top. This layer is beneficial to the melting process as it helps to keep out oxygen and other gases. When you're ready to add cans or other thin aluminum, drop them into your crucible then push them immediately through this slag layer with your slag spoon before they oxidize. You will save lots of aluminum using this method instead of starting with cans.

Another advantage of mixing thick pieces in with your cans and thin aluminum is that most thick aluminum will be alloyed with complimentary metals that add strength and machinability. In contrast, the aluminum used for drink cans and other thin material is often alloyed with materials to make it easier to roll into flat, thin sheets. These sorts of alloys, while strong for pressure containers, are not as easy to machine and will be more likely to gum up drill bits and files when you finish the parts. So always add some thick pieces to every melt to ensure better machinability than only cans would provide.

Use the Table of Aluminum Alloys in Appendix A to help you sort your scrap for ideal mixes. As you practice melting aluminum and pouring it into ingots in your cupcake pans, try to keep alloys separated and mark your resulting ingots with their content. Even though you will start your drink can melting with thick pieces, these few pieces will not be the majority of the melt, so you can mark those ingots as made from cans and sheet. Other alloys come in thick pieces that can start your melts for their ingots. This separation will allow you to organize your ingots and create the best mixes when you are ready for casting into your mold. Keep in mind that each of the eight alloy series has several sub-alloys, for example 2024, 6061, and 7075 are some common ones. These sub-alloys combine other alloying elements, so the table notes are general characteristics that run through each series. Sub-alloys will have minor variations, but these are not important to learn for your basic sorting purposes. Create at least three categories:

1. drink cans, foil, and sheet metal (1xxx, 2xxx, 3xxx wrought, and 5xxx);
2. cast (3xxx cast and 4xxx); and
3. bike and motorcycle parts, bike frames, aircraft parts, and extruded (6xxx and 7xxx)

By sorting your scrap and ingots into at least these three categories you can determine the basic alloy composition of each of your melts and have a better chance of refining your process. For instance, the first category includes cans and sheet metal that are very ductile and easy to work. This can make your shift levers resilient to certain loads, but it also makes the aluminum soft, which can gum up your files and drill bits during finishing. The second category with cast parts will bring in the silicon used in production casting that improves flow of the molten metal to ensure it reaches all corners of your mold. The third category brings in alloys used for higher strength that also improve machinability, but don't flow as well as the sheet or production cast aluminum.

The first category is often the most prevalent scrap found so you will likely need to include quite a bit of it in each pour simply to use the scrap you obtain. Then add to each pour some from each of the other categories in order to improve your cast as well as the strength and machinability of your shift levers.

Keep pushing pieces and cans into your molten mix until you have a bit more molten metal than you need for your pour. When pouring ingots, you can nearly fill your crucible. Stir the molten metal just a bit and scrape the bottom to ensure the slag is separating from the aluminum and your crucible. Most slag, especially slag from oxidation, is buoyant in molten aluminum, which is why it generally stays at the top. Some slag bits will settle at the bottom of your crucible, but these are usually nonaluminum inclusions like sand, steel, or other metals with higher melting temperatures. A gentle stir along with a good scrape of the bottom will separate these slag elements from your molten aluminum.

Pure slag will be dry, dull, and dusty, but if it still contains a significant amount of aluminum it will look and feel more like a silvery sponge when you press it against the side of your crucible with your slag spoon. In fact, pressing it like this can actually wring out some of that aluminum. Slag will also tend to turn red hot before molten aluminum. At a proper melting point for aluminum, slag is easy to distinguish as it will be bright red and your aluminum will still be silver or only slightly pinkish.

Wring out as much aluminum as you can, then remove the majority of the remaining slag, placing it into a separate steel bowl or a cupcake pan. Any remaining slag, as long is there is not much, will tend to cling to the side of your crucible as you pour. Don’t remove your slag until you are ready to pour because the top of the exposed molten aluminum will oxidize and create more slag. This wastes aluminum. Keep your slag layer intact as protection against oxidation until just before you pour.

Before pouring, make sure your aluminum is ready. You do not want to keep it molten for too long as it will eventually start to degrade as gases like hydrogen find their way in, but you also must ensure it is hot enough to flow well into all corners of the mold. One way to tell when it's hot enough is that it will no longer stick to your slag spoon. You may also note a bit of pink at the edges, but try to avoid it getting red hot as it is more vulnerable to detrimental gases in this state. Whenever you see your aluminum is red hot, immediately add some cold pieces to bring the temperature back down. Note how often your aluminum reaches the red hot state. If it happens every pour, your air supply is likely too powerful. Ask your workers to take it easier with a hand pump or set your electrical blower to a lower setting.

When the molten metal is just right, it will pour as freely as cream. Once it cools down to a less fluid state and starts sticking to your spoon again, increase the air supply to make your coals hotter. You may also need to add more coals below and along the sides of your crucible. Hot coals should surround the crucible all the way to the top edge to ensure an even melt and prevent cooling and sticking at the top. Keeping the lid on longer will retain the heat and allow the aluminum to reach the ideal temperature. The coals will smoke when the temperature is too low. Right when they stop smoking they will have reached a good heat for melting.

Do several practice melts, before pouring into your mold. This will familiarize you with your furnace and help you get a feel for melting and pouring efficiently. Add these details to your employee training notes to streamline their training. Keep track of the amount of charcoal you're using and the energy needed to pump, noting ways to improve efficiency either by keeping the lid on longer or changing the volume of air—too much will burn through charcoal faster than needed, too little will take longer to reach the melting point. Also note the energy and charcoal needed in the separate fire pit or BBQ along with any increase of efficiency after preheating your crucible and scrap before moving them to the furnace.

Pour these practice melts into your cupcake pans to make handy ingots that you can melt again. These cupcake pans are also a good place to pour extra metal after you've finished pouring into your mold. Mark such ingots with their particular mix and store them separately if you don't use them that day. Never let aluminum solidify in your crucible as it will expand when reheated and could break the crucible.

Also practice re-melting any slag you think retained significant amounts of aluminum. Pure slag will be dull and darker than aluminum and behave more like a dusty, flaky mass that can be easily crumbled in your hands. Slag that contains a lot of shiny silver and holds together in a hard clump may be worth melting again to see if some more aluminum will separate and flow away from the slag. Gauge the time and amount of charcoal it takes to re-melt your slag to determine when it is worth it or not. A few streaks of silver in a mostly dull dusty mass will likely not justify it. However, a very silvery clump of slag can be a useful way to start your melt, especially for melting cans. Since you need a layer of slag through which you can push your cans, a slag re-melt that contains ample aluminum provides this needed layer as well as a nice pool of molten aluminum to consume the first cans.

Making ingots can become a regular practice in order to keep your stockpile of scrap manageable and increase efficiency on production days. This works especially well for drink cans and sheet metal because they are the most common scrap and they take up far more space than thicker pieces. Thick pieces are easy enough to store once they are cut down to crucible-size and can be added directly to your melt. Also, because cans and sheet aluminum create more slag than other types, that slag can be removed while making ingots so your workers won't have to bother with so much slag on production days. These ingots then become a nice way to start each melt.

Once you're comfortable working with this hot molten stuff and you have set up your foundry to your liking, it's time to try pouring into your mold. Melt only about twice as much metal as you need for your pour. Molten aluminum degrades over time as hydrogen, oxygen, and other elements find their way into the inviting fluid. To keep degradation of your molten aluminum to a minimum, melt quickly then pour all of that batch, either into your mold or cupcake pans, before starting a new batch.

With just one mold, there's no need to fill your crucible more than halfway. Make sure to melt about twice as much as you need in order to avoid pouring only a partial part. This will also avoid allowing heavy slag to flow from the bottom of your crucible into your mold. After pouring into the mold, pour the remaining aluminum into your cupcake pan to cool as an ingot that can be melted again. Then you can add charcoal to your furnace, replace your empty crucible, add big pieces or ingots, start your pool, add more, and keep it going.

SUMMARY OF SAFETY TIPS

- Keep molten aluminum away from concrete as the moisture contained in the concrete will explode on contact.
- Foundry workers need to wear a full cover of natural fiber clothing; never synthetics as they are flammable. Eye protection should also be required.
- Keep water and moisture away from molten aluminum as it explodes on contact.
- Dry drink cans completely before melting.
- If a roof is necessary over the furnace, leave walls off to ensure proper ventilation of carbon monoxide from charcoal and paint fumes from melting scrap.
- Symptoms of overexposure to toxins include confusion, weakness, and speech problems. If recovery is slow, seek medical attention.
- Zinc fumes are toxic so remove it from scrap.
- Magnesium burns explosively so remove it from scrap.
- When using electrical cutting and finishing tools, never use an abrasive cutting blade or grinding wheel on aluminum. Instead use toothed blades or a belt sander.

In the next chapter we will look at producing and finishing Bike Shift Levers, including tips for any product. The focus will be on using the Bike Shift Lever mold and the accompanying jig, but much of that process will transfer to the use of any mold. Now that you understand the basics, your casting opportunities are endless.

Chapter 4

Production and Finishing

This chapter focuses on the use of the Bike Shift Lever permanent mold and its accompanying jig for finishing each part as guidance for our license partners. The mold is quite simple to use as long as your foundry is well set up and your workers have practiced melting aluminum with it. Even so, this chapter covers important steps as well as details to follow in order to ensure every casting comes out as a high quality shift lever.

Readers looking to become one of our license partners and establish a profitable operation manufacturing Bike Shift Levers will need to produce a good stockpile before attempting to sell them. You may be anxious to get the word out about your shifters and prepare people to buy them as soon as the aluminum cools. But this will only set you and your customers up for frustration. Developing a smooth production line and system for sales takes some trial and error. Also, you cannot know the actual direct cost per shift lever until you have produced quite a few and found average expenses as you and your employees work out kinks in your system. Plan for this patient, quiet beginning as you learn and practice using your mold. Later in this book you will read about calculating costs and settling on a profitable price for your shift levers that keeps them affordable for your customers even as it supports your operation well into the future.

For readers who are not interested in becoming a license partner in order to receive one of our permanent molds, you will still find interesting information that would apply to the use of any mold for other items. There are many other ways to make things using aluminum casting once you understand these basic principles.

In case you simply want to make a few Bike Shift Levers or try your hand at a different product, you have several alternative mold options.

Sand casting is popular for producing just a few of a particular item. It becomes tedious, though, when trying to make the same item repeatedly because a whole new mold must be created before each pour. For a small, detailed item like the Bike Shift Lever, great care must be given to preparing the sand and carefully brushing away any stray sand grains that could distort holes or leave gaps that would disrupt the function of the shift lever.

You may still be interested in pursuing sand casting if you only want to make a few Bike Shift Levers for yourself or you are looking to make various other items with your foundry. Once you set up a sand casting foundry, you can cast just about anything that has a simple form and edges that allow the pattern to be removed from the mold prior to casting. You will also need to learn pattern making in order to create the proper indentation in the sand that results in the item you want to make.

Lost wax is another type of casting that requires the mold to be broken after each casting, allowing more complex items to be cast this way. Because the mold is destroyed after each casting, lost wax is generally not used for making the same piece many times. However, bronze casters and other metal artists prefer this casting method because it allows intricate, undercut details that would prevent them from being removed from other types of molds.

You can find lots of instruction for sand and lost wax casting mold and pattern design on the internet. Also in the Resources section of this book you will find recommended books and internet links that cover these casting techniques.

USING THE BIKE SHIFT LEVER PERMANENT MOLD

Unlike sand and lost wax casting, casting with a permanent mold allows quick, repeated pours of the same item. As soon as the molten metal solidifies, the mold can be opened, the part removed, the mold reassembled, and more metal poured. A permanent mold is meant to last for many, many castings before it needs to be replaced.

The Bike Shift Lever permanent mold is made of steel, comes in two halves, and includes both the lever and base of the shift lever. Before attempting your first pour into the mold, recheck your foundry setup to ensure all is in order. Check that there is a flat area near your furnace where the mold can be laid without danger of it tipping over. A level area of bricks (never concrete!) would work well. Stand at your furnace and do several mock pours into your mold with your crucible cold and empty. Watch where your feet must move and look for anything that might trip the pourer or distract them in anyway. Remove all obstacles and make adjustments to the arrangements to ensure a smooth easy movement for every pour.

Study your mold when it arrives. You will recognize the indents for each of the parts and see how the parting line between the halves travels along each part to ensure

they can be removed from the mold. At the top of the mold you will see two funnel shapes. These are called the sprues and are where you will pour the molten aluminum. To the sides, you will see vents that allow air and gases to escape as the aluminum descends into the mold. Each part has several holes for cables and bolts. You'll see that some of these holes are managed by protrusions in each side of the mold coming together when it is assembled. These holes will require some cleanup after they are cast. The bolt hole for the lever is created in a different way—with a core pin—and should not need much clean up.

Your Bike Shift Lever mold comes with several important parts. These are fairly common, so if they are lost or broken, you should be able to purchase them in your area. If you have trouble finding replacement parts, you can also purchase them from us. Look for these parts in the package that arrives:

- Permanent mold, two halves
- Core pins to create hole in lever, including extra; same size as register pins in case those need to be replaced (one inch (2.5cm) long, 1/4 inch (6mm) diameter).
- Two long bolts with wing nuts for clamping mold together (any size that fits will work).

Before assembling your mold for each pour, lay both halves over an opening so their insides face down.

Hold a candle under each so that its flame covers each cavity and the flat surfaces with black soot. This carbon coating will help prevent the parts from sticking and will make them easier to remove from the mold. It will also make it easier to open the mold. Then clasp a core pin with pliers and hold it over the candle flame until it is entirely covered in black soot. This will make it easier to remove from the mold and then from the lever.

A low-flame cutting torch will also work to coat your mold and core pin with carbon. Another option is to purchase a carbon or graphite release agent from a casting supply store if one is nearby. These release agents do the same job as a candle or torch flame, but may be easier to apply.

Before inserting your core pin into its notch in either side of the mold, run your fingers along it to make sure it has not acquired any rough spots. Sometimes your punch will flatten the end of the pin as you drive it out of a lever. The lip caused by this flattening will cause the pin to catch inside the next lever if you don't find it beforehand. Simply file off such a lip or other rough spot and then smooth it with fine sandpaper before coating it and inserting it into the mold.

The mold has two register pins in its corners to guide the halves together. In the other two corners you will see a through hole. These holes are where you will insert the two bolts for clamping with the wing nuts. Tighten the wing nuts as much as you can using only your hand. No need to over tighten with tools. After tightening the wing nuts, check for even the slightest gap between the halves. If you see a gap that cannot be closed by tightening the wing nuts, open the mold and look for debris that might be preventing the halves from meeting.

As you prepare to cast your first Bike Shift Lever,

know that even with all the care you've taken, your first pours are likely to have some flaws. We'll look at causes of defects later in this chapter, but for now, realize that it takes some practice to get everything right. Don't worry about flawed castings. All you have to do is drop them back into your crucible to melt again and have another chance at perfection.

After assembling your mold with your coated core pin in place and your wing nuts tightened to close gaps all around the mold, you will need to place the mold entirely into your furnace for preheating. The mold needs to reach the same temperature as the molten aluminum—about

1,200°F (660°C)—to allow the aluminum to flow to all corners of the parts evenly and without cooling along the way. Because the mold is made of steel, which melts at about 2,600°F (1,450°C), it may get a bit red, but will not distort. Still, it will be extremely hot; too hot to pick up with even the thickest leather gloves.

You will see a loop at the top of the mold that is designed for large pliers or any sort of strong steel rod or hooking device for removing it from your furnace. Locate such pliers or a steel hook before preheating the mold and do some practice runs to make sure it works well for placing the mold into the furnace and then removing it.

Depending on your furnace setup and how much ash is blown upward when you start your pump or blower, you may want to cover the sprues of your mold with a flat piece of steel. This will prevent ash from entering the mold and causing imperfections in your shift levers. Make sure this piece of steel overhangs or has a protrusion that you can grasp with pliers to remove it just before pouring.

The last preparation steps before even starting the charcoal should be to ensure all of your safety gear and devices are in place. Check that your water supply is in easy reach in case a fire spreads (but remind everyone to keep water away from the molten aluminum). Place shovels and loose sand or dirt nearby to extinguish a fire near the furnace. And most importantly, make sure that every foundry worker is covered from head to toe with natural-fiber clothing such as cotton, leather, or wool—hat, long sleeves, thick leather gloves, long pants or skirt, socks, and shoes. These will protect them not only from the extreme heat, but potential splatters of the molten metal. Each worker should also have a pair of safety glasses in case moisture enters the crucible and causes the molten aluminum to burst upward. These glasses are also important for preparing the aluminum and finishing the parts as cutting, pounding, filing, and grinding can throw pieces into eyes. If you use an electric chop saw, as described earlier, or any other power tools for preparing aluminum or finishing parts, add ear muffs to protect your workers' ears.

Once you are confident with your preheating

procedure, you and your workers are covered in safe clothing and gear, and all of your foundry tools and elements are in place, it's time to start the charcoal. Follow the directions described earlier for melting aluminum. This time, you may have enough ingots and clean aluminum that you won't have to deal with paint fumes or even much slag. This is another benefit of creating ingots with your scrap—on casting days you can work with clean aluminum.

The Bike Shift Lever parts take very little aluminum. Total for both parts is about half of an ingot made in a typical cupcake pan. So you only need to melt about two ingots or the equivalent for each pour. By melting two ingots you will have enough to pour past your slag and won't have to empty your crucible into the mold, which could include slag from the bottom. You can pour the leftover aluminum into your cupcake pan to be ready for the next melt.

Hopefully you were a bit organized as you made your ingots and marked them with their likely alloy content using the Table of Aluminum Alloys in Appendix A. As mentioned earlier, try to mix your alloys to avoid too much from cans and sheet metal because these are more difficult to drill and finish as they tend to gum up tools. At the same time, avoid too much from extruded items and bike parts as these alloys are harder and may not flow as well into the mold. If you have plenty of cast aluminum scraps, be sure to mix some of these into your melts. The silicon content of these production castings will help the flow of your pours.

When you see that your molten aluminum is just turning pink and it no longer sticks to your slag spoon it is ready to pour. Remove the ash cap from your mold and keep the mold in the furnace for the pour. Skim any slag off the top, stop the air supply, lift your crucible, and pour it into the two sprues at the top of your mold in one smooth motion. Pour slowly, but without hesitation to prevent the aluminum cooling as it enters the sprues. You'll be surprised at how little goes into each sprue before it billows up. Pour until a small cushion forms above the sprue, then keep pouring just a bit to ensure that part receives ample aluminum. Then move immediately to the next sprue before the aluminum cools. You should fill both parts in just a few seconds.

After each sprue is filled, pour the remaining molten metal into your cupcake pan to make new ingots that will be warm and ready for your next melt. Again, don't let the aluminum solidify in your crucible because it could crack it as it expands during the next melt. Also, by pouring the aluminum out into your cupcake pan, you can scrape out any heavy slag that collected in the bottom of your crucible.

Remove the mold from the furnace and allow the parts to cool in your for at least 15 minutes before unscrewing the wing nuts and opening the mold. Use this time to start the next melt. Adjust the remaining coals and place your crucible in the middle, adding new coals all around it, leaving a spot open for the mold once it's ready again. Start your air supply and add the warm ingots to your crucible plus some more scrap, keeping the alloy mix about the same. Place the lid over the furnace for a faster melt. You'll likely have a few more minutes before it's time to open the mold. Use this time to organize the area and prepare for later pours. Once you've cast several shift levers, this time can be used to inspect and begin finishing the parts if you only have a few workers on the job.

Opening the mold can be a bit difficult until you get the hang of it. When it is sufficiently cooled, lay it on its side, unscrew the wing nuts, remove the bolts, and use a wedge-shaped tool to pry it open. Any sort of thick chisel or even a hatchet will work well. You may need to tap the chisel or hatchet with a hammer to encourage the halves to separate. If you do need to use a hammer, be careful that your tool does not enter the mold so far that it hits the parts. Flip the mold back and forth, creating a small gap on one side, then a similar gap on the other until the gap clears the register pins. At this point you should be able to wiggle and lift one half away from the other with your gloved hand.

Carefully use your pliers to remove each part without scarring the parts with the pliers' teeth. Once each of the parts is out of the mold you only need to remove the core pin from the lever before they are ready for inspection and finishing. Lay the lever over the jaws of your vise with just enough of a gap for the pin to fit between. Two bricks will also work in a similar way. Use a steel punch or large nail with your hammer to tap the core pin out of the lever.

Once the parts are out of the mold and you've retrieved and inspected the core pin, you can blacken the mold and pin again, place the pin into the mold, assemble the mold, and place it into your furnace for preheating. The aluminum you placed into your crucible to melt as you were removing the parts should be getting close to ready. As you practice this system of melt, pour, melt, remove, and so on, you and your workers will begin to find a rhythm that gains efficiency each time.

Another way to increase efficiency is to add more molds to your operation. This way you can fill your crucible with more aluminum and pour more parts each time. Or you could have one mold in the furnace as the other cools. Contact us when you think you are ready to purchase more molds.

QUALITY INSPECTION

Carefully inspect every part you cast before wasting time preparing, assembling, and packaging defective parts.

Discovering flaws and defects at the furnace will save valuable time and avoid returned shifters from unhappy customers. Note each defect and its likely cause before re-melting these flawed parts. By taking careful notes you will discover important patterns and identify problems to be remedied before more occur.

Defects in parts can occur in several different forms. You might find a void where aluminum should have filled. Sometimes a part will have cracked. Other times you'll find holes or inclusions of sand grains or other foreign matter.

Odd-shaped voids that are much larger than a pin hole either within the body of the part or at its extremities are often caused by pouring aluminum that is not hot enough or pouring into a mold that was not properly preheated. When the aluminum cools before reaching the part's extremities, you'll find rounded or missing corners and misshaped parts. Voids within the body of the part occur when the aluminum cools prematurely in other areas blocking the flow and then pulling the molten aluminum from that area.

Cold shuts are also caused by temperatures that are too low. These are places where the aluminum was supposed to flow around a core or protrusion and rejoin on the other side. Instead, because the aluminum or mold was not hot enough, the aluminum freezes before rejoining leaving a break or even a gap.

If you find voids or cold shuts in your castings, spend more time preheating your mold and ensuring the aluminum is ready for pouring. Aluminum is ready to pour when it starts to turn a bit pink and it no longer sticks to your slag spoon. Properly heated aluminum pours as easily as cream.

If voids and cold shuts continue to appear even after proper heating, you may be using too much of the 6xxx and

7xxx alloy series in your pours. These are usually extruded pieces as well as most scrap from bicycles, motorcycles, and airplanes. These alloys are known for strength, but don't flow as well as the others. Try mixing in more can and sheet alloys plus as much cast alloy scrap as you can. The cast alloys, 3xxx and 4xxx will always offer the best flow. Unfortunately, they are less common in most parts of the world and difficult to reduce into small enough pieces to fit your crucible. Still, adding just a few pieces of cast scrap to your pours will help the flow and help to remedy voids and cold shuts.

Gas bubbles leave small holes where gases such as hydrogen were trapped. When this defect is showing up it usually means that you have been letting your aluminum stay liquid too long. Hydrogen is attracted to molten aluminum and will find its way into your pour if you give it enough time. Wet climates will have more trouble with hydrogen inclusions than dry climates because of the humidity in the air. Another cause could be blocked vents either from debris or spillage from your pours.

Inclusions of ash, sand, slag, or other foreign matter cause weaknesses in a casting because they do not adhere to the aluminum. They act much like a void or gas bubble and can make the part vulnerable to breaking at that spot. Such inclusions happen when not enough aluminum was melted and slag was not properly skimmed off the top. Also, if you notice ash blowing into your sprues, this could be the culprit. Cover your sprues with a flat piece of steel before the next pour.

Light slag such as that formed from oxidation, floats to the top of the melt. You can easily skim most of it off with your slag spoon prior to pouring. As long as most is skimmed off, any remaining light slag will tend to stick to the sides of your crucible and let the aluminum pour past.

But if this slag layer is thick and not skimmed off before pouring, some will flow into the pour and create a weak inclusion.

When not enough aluminum was melted, the pourer will have to tip the crucible too far in order to fill the mold. This allows sand and other heavy slag that collects at the bottom of the crucible to flow into the mold and create inclusions. Train your workers to melt more than enough aluminum for each pour and properly skim slag to avoid inclusions.

Other defects occur because of poor mold design. We have designed the Bike Shift Lever mold to avoid such defects, but if you create your own molds either with the sand casting or lost wax processes, you might discover some of these.

Hot tears occur when the cooling metal cannot contract without tearing apart. They look like jagged cracks or tears through the casting. Hot tears are often caused by poor mold design, but they also occur if not enough aluminum was poured into the sprue. If the cushion that forms at the top of the mold is sucked down and turns into a funnel shape, you may find a hot tear in the part when you open the mold. As you pour, make sure the cushion forms fully before moving on to the next sprue.

A poorly designed mold can also cause distortions when thick areas cool slower than adjacent thin areas. Design can also contribute to voids and cold shuts when the molten metal is required to travel through complex shapes and sharp corners. If you plan to make your own molds, spend quality time learning proper mold design to avoid such defects in your castings.

FINISHING THE PARTS & USING THE JIG

Finishing the cast parts starts with carefully removing them from the mold and removing the core pin from the lever. The more careful you are, the less finishing you will have to do to remove scars made by any tools you use. Next, twist or hacksaw off the extra aluminum that extended into the vents and hacksaw off each sprue. Jagged edges left from these removals can be easily filed off with a file. If you have electrical tools, a band saw and belt sander work well for these jobs. Also clean up any rough edges around the parting line or other places aluminum may have strayed. This is also a good time to look for any defects that may have been missed at the furnace.

Your vise can be used to hold the parts for filing and cleaning out the holes that were made during casting, but first add two pieces of sheet aluminum that fold over the vise's jaws. Because aluminum is softer than steel, these vise jaw covers will allow you to clamp each part tightly without leaving scars.

Next the remaining holes will have to be drilled carefully to ensure that the shifter operates properly. When you first sign up to be a license partner to produce Bike Shift Levers, you will receive a special jig along with your first mold. You can also purchase more of these jigs from us if this first one wears out or you want to expand your finishing operation. This jig performs three jobs:

- To hold the base for the drilling of the two cable holes and the accompanying recesses that hold and stop the cable housing.
- To hold the bottle cap and punch a centered hole.
- To hold the hose clamp for punching a hole then tapping its sides to fit snuggly around the base.

There may be instances when this jig is not available, for instance during remote field repairs or when parts must be cast in less-than-ideal conditions in order to get a customer back on the road. Drilling of the cable and housing holes into the base will be the most difficult, but not impossible. Start with the small hole and do your best to hold the angle of your drill to ensure the cable can enter the base from the front of the bike without kinking. The cable hole must exit the base to line the cable up with the groove in the lever (make sure to account for the space needed for the hose clamp below the lever). Next, follow the small hole with the larger drill bit to create the housing hole. Drill this hole just deep enough that it will stabilize the housing.

For normal finishing you will use your jig. It will guide each drill bit to the correct spot and angle and ensure the punched holes are nicely centered. Your jig will come with detailed instructions to help you and your workers perform each task quickly and with ease.

The hole in the bottle cap can be easily punched with a large nail even without the jig as long as it is centered. An easy way to find the center is to place inside the cap a washer that just fits and has a small hole. Tap your punch or nail inside this small hole to form a guide for the through punch after removing the washer.

The hole in the hose clamp is also easy to punch with a punch or large nail. Just make sure it is centered and that you choose a spot that leaves the screw mechanism facing forward when installed on the bike. This prevents that screw mechanism from injuring the rider's leg during hard pedaling or the rider's hand when moving around the handlebar.

ASSEMBLY

By this time, you should have ordered a good quantity of the bolts, nuts, hose clamps, and bottle caps needed to complete your shift levers. Once all six parts are prepared, each shifter should be ready for assembly. Place a nut into the hex recess in the bottom of a base, insert the bolt into the cap hole then the lever hole, the clamp hole, and finally the base hole. Tighten the bolt into the nut using your 7/16" or 11mm wrench until it compresses all parts.

You will read in the next chapter about wearing in your shift levers before packaging them for sale. For now, it's time to celebrate—you have just produced your first Bike Shift Lever!

Now let's move on to how these shifters function and their attributes so you can create a successful sales operation. In the next chapter you will learn not only about installing and using these shift levers, but pricing them properly and marketing them to your most likely customers.

Chapter 5

Installation and Sales

Once you've stockpiled a good number of assembled shift levers, you should be ready to start selling them. Before you start spreading the word, though, there are quite a few other considerations you and your team will want to take care of first. By covering these details in advance, you will create a smooth sales system that reaches as many customers as possible, sets a price that brings a profit, and keeps a steady flow of shifters filling the demand that results from your marketing.

The Bike Shift Lever's simplicity and unique features make for an exciting product that can attract many types of customers. For instance, it is the first symmetrical shift lever made for bicycles that we know of. This means that it can be used on either the right or left sides to shift either the rear or front derailleur.

Some of your potential customers may be tired of having to replace their fragile, race-designed shift levers every few months. Others will be desperate for an affordable, repairable shift lever that will hold up to hard use. The Bike Shift Lever is designed for people who ride daily and enables them to repair their shift lever themselves. All of these qualities can be spot lit in your marketing material and offered to your customers who come to you for a great shift lever.

This chapter will look at these features, tips on installing these shift levers onto bikes, and many of the sales considerations you and your team will have to prepare for in order to do a good job selling this as well as other products.

FUNCTION OF THE BIKE SHIFT LEVER

One important and unique quality of the Bike Shift Lever is that it is designed with very common, basic parts so that it can be repaired easily and in many different ways. Four of these parts—the bottle cap, hose clamp, bolt and nut—are not designed or produced specifically for this shift lever. This means that they all need a bit of time to wear in and settle into their new function as Bike Shift Lever parts. The aluminum of the other two parts, which you will cast in your foundry, is soft enough to allow these parts to settle into place and even allows for variations in different styles of clamps and bottle caps.

Once the shift lever is worn in, the spring strength of the stainless steel hose clamp causes the friction needed to hold the cable in one gear. This spring action pushes the lever away from the base and against the bolt head allowing for fine tuning of the tension with the bolt. Before these parts have settled in, the shift lever will tend to slip and not hold that friction. All that is needed is a slight tightening of the bolt to compress the parts together. This can often be accomplished without a wrench, just using fingers.

The bottle cap needs to be flat before it will behave as a slippery washer rather than catching and unscrewing the bolt. This is why proper preparation of your bottle caps is important prior to assembly. But even a well-prepared bottle cap will need a bit of wear-in time. A slight bolt tightening may cause it to catch, but follow that by pushing and pulling the lever several times and it will free itself. Then repeat this process with a bolt turn, push and pull a few more times and it should find its sweet spot.

The hose clamp also goes through a break-in process. Even after being properly hole-punched and pounded on the sides, it will still need some time to settle into the aluminum it rests against. As the aluminum wears against it and the stainless steel flattens, space will free up and allow slippage. Again, tightening the bolt then pushing and pulling the lever several times should take care of this.

It's a good idea to include in your assembly process some artificial wear-in procedure so that your customers will only have to tighten their Bike Shift Lever bolt a few times before it holds their gears without slipping. Have your workers mount each shift lever to a handlebar or horizontal pipe in order to do this bolt tightening and pushing and pulling on each lever before they are packaged.

Another unique quality of the Bike Shift Lever is that it is symmetrical. In order to make it symmetrical, the design includes two different cable holes on the base and allows the cable to be threaded through the lever both ways.

When installing the shifter onto a bike, make sure to insert the cable housing into the hole that causes the housing to loop toward the front of the bike without sharp bends. Then thread the cable into the lever cable hole in the direction that feeds the cable directly into that housing hole when the lever points toward the rider—the position when the cable will be slack. When the correct cable hole and cable direction are chosen, the cable will travel the shortest distance and will have no sharp bends even when the lever is moved to shift into the farthest gear.

PACKAGING

We recommend keeping your packaging to a minimum. Not only does minimal packaging follow the principles of the project by keeping waste low, it will also save your operation significant money over time. Even so, your packaging should look professional and give your potential customers a clear message that this is a quality product with a proud organization behind it.

One Street offers packaging designs and graphics for our license partners. Our partners can download these designs, adjust them to their needs, and send them on to their local print shop for easy printing.

PRICING AND DISTRIBUTION

The budget you began in Chapter 2 will become the basis of your pricing process for your Bike Shift Levers. In order to do its job of showing you the actual cost of each shift lever you manufacture, you will need to include every expense. Start with the List of Supplies and Resources in Chapter 2. Many of these will be one-time purchases, so you can note them as capital investments. Even so, you want the profit from your shift lever sales to return that money over time. Also add all other expenses that you have encountered including license and renewal fees. Your organization will have to subsidize these expenses at the start, but plan to pay back these subsidies with the profits from sales. Once these capital expenses are paid back, designate future profits to cover the overhead expenses that keep your foundry operational so that you will minimize the impact to your other programs.

Find your direct costs to manufacture each shift lever by calculating all the ongoing expenses needed to produce them. Start with expenses for casting the two aluminum parts including employee wages. Then add the cost of the bolt, nut, bottle cap, and hose clamp for each. Add to that the cost of your employees to finish, assemble and prepare the shifter for sale, including the cost of packaging.

Calculate the number of shift levers you can manufacture from bulk purchases such as charcoal and transportation of scrap aluminum. Then divide these expenses by that number to note that particular direct cost per shift lever.

Don't forget to include the cost to deliver each shift lever to the place where it will be sold. You may sell some right at your foundry, but most will be sold elsewhere.

Once you've added up all direct costs to determine the cost to manufacture and sell each shift lever, round that number up to allow for inevitable mishaps and hidden expenses you will have missed. By carefully calculating and noting every expense that goes into production, then adding this contingency, you will find the correct direct cost per shift lever. In the United States, this direct cost per product is often called cost of goods sold.

Sometimes you will be lucky enough to receive a large donation of scrap aluminum delivered to your door or perhaps charcoal and other supplies. Do not lower your estimated cost per shift lever to accommodate such donations. Your cost per shift lever needs to be calculated using ongoing purchases you will have to make when such donations are not available. Donations cannot be relied upon, so your estimated cost per shifter should reflect the more likely scenario of purchasing the materials and resources needed to make them. The same goes for volunteers who may donate their time to help cast or assemble your shift levers. Volunteers rarely stay for long and often leave jobs partially done. Instead, view donations of materials and time as fortunate boosts to your operation that will contribute to a buffer to cover unexpected setbacks that always seem to happen, no matter how carefully you plan.

Most manufactures follow the rule that retail price is at least four times as much as the direct costs to produce their product. This allows for even your wholesale price to cover not just the direct cost of each shifter, but some of your overhead, your unexpected expenses, and finally some profit. In the bike industry and most other retail industries, wholesale price is half of retail. In an ideal world, you would sell all of your shifters directly to the end customer at retail. Unfortunately, you are unlikely to have that much reach, especially when you are focusing so much of your time and resources on manufacturing.

Realize that most of the shifters you manufacture will have to be sold through other retailers. They will purchase them from you at your wholesale price so they can sell them at retail. Even supplying retailers in your region will be an enormous job. First you have to convince them to stock your shift levers, then take their orders, then fill their orders, then invoice them, and follow up for payments and reorders. Of course this is better than personally talking with every single customer who buys one, but not by much.

So you may need to work with distributors that serve retailers in your area. Think of distributors as another layer in your sales channel who will also need to make some money from the sale. Fortunately, since all they have to do is receive your product then ship it to retailers, they don't expect to take much from each sale. They deal in volume, which is how they make their money as well as save you an enormous amount of time and effort not having to deal with each and every retailer.

Designate specific prices for each of these three sales channels by starting with your base cost to produce and deliver one shift lever. Here's an example of how such a pricing breakdown might look:

- Cost to manufacture, assemble, package and deliver each shift lever: $4.00
- Price to sell to distributors: $6.00
- Wholesale price that retailers pay: $8.00
- Retail price that customers pay: $16.00

Your price to distributors will be the lowest, but should result in your highest volume of sales, which offsets that low price by reducing your overhead cost per sale. Next, your wholesale price to retailers should be about half of your retail price. These wholesale sales will require quite a bit more time and administration than distributor sales, so balance this with the amount of effort you put into obtaining and dealing with such wholesale accounts. You will also sell shift levers directly to customers at retail. These better sales margins will help make up for the distributor pricing and contribute to overhead costs required to keep your foundry and organization going.

Your direct sales to customers will likely be your lowest volume of sales and will always be the most time consuming to accommodate. At least each retail sale will bring the best profit margin and help the most in covering your overhead costs. Discuss with your team the various ways you can sell at retail without compromising your manufacturing operations. If your website can take orders, this could be a great way to add retail sales to your lineup. Then your employees can fill these internet sales when time allows such as before or after foundry operations or on days when casting and assembly are not needed.

While the price to your distributors will look mighty deflating, remember that their potential volume of sales will make up for it as demand for your shifters grows. If you decide to work with distributors, make a point of filling their orders immediately even as you know they are receiving them at such a low price. By keeping your relationship strong, they will continue to publish their catalogs with your shift levers included as in-stock, ready to order. The volume of orders will increase over time and what you miss in individual profits per item will be made up in volume as you take their large checks to the bank.

If you decide to work with distributors as part of your Bike Shift Lever sales strategy, check with us before reaching out to any. We can help you find the best distributors to work with in your area and avoid abusive distributors who demand bigger discounts and present products poorly. We can also check to see if other license partners are or are planning to sell Bike Shift Levers through these same distributors, in which case we can help you find untapped sales channels that will serve your needs. There may also be an opportunity to partner with these other licensees to supply Bike Shift Levers to these distributors as well as promote the shifters to increase demand and sales.

One more consideration regarding working with distributors is that they may require you to purchase product liability insurance before they will consider carrying your product in their catalog. Such a policy covers any damages or injuries that might be caused by your product and reassures your distributors (and even your retailers) that they will not be sued for damages by the people who buy the product. In the United States, a product liability policy costs about $350 annually for a small manufacturing operation such as this. Other, less lawsuit-obsessed countries may not even bother with these policies. If you do run into this requirement from your potential distributors, be sure to divide the annual policy fee by the likely number of shifters you'll sell each year and add this cost to your cost for each shift lever.

Hold fast to your pricing plan so that distributors always pay their price, retailers always pay full wholesale price, and customers always pay full retail. Never undercut your own prices. Keep a lookout to ensure your retailers do not discount them. Setting a price has to be firm or you will not cover your overhead and unexpected expenses. Profit is rarely pure profit. Most profits go toward covering overhead, mishaps, and unexpected expenses. When these are taken care of, profits then go toward stockpiling inventory to fill future orders.

As your product manufacturing operation matures, mishaps and unexpected expenses should diminish as you and your team shift the unexpected into expected expenses and increase your per shifter price accordingly. Mishaps will also become rarities as your team settles into an efficient routine. As these improvements take place, profits can finally be invested in growing the operation including increasing promotions, outreach to more wholesale accounts, and even adding sales staff to sell direct to customers. Eventually, some of your profits may even support other programs your organization is undertaking.

Don't make the mistake of considering profits to be "extra" money to play with. Instead, profits are your only means of ensuring your Bike Shift Lever manufacturing can continue and thrive. Every dollar (or equivalent) you make above the cost to make and deliver each shifter should be used with the greatest care to keep your operation producing at full speed and finding ways to improve. Focus on making your foundry a successful program that supports your employees and produces great shift levers before moving any of its profits into other programs.

Unless you are doing this as a hobby, you cannot afford to sacrifice your foundry and organization to discounts. If any of your team members argue for discounting to particular customers or for other reasons, remind them of the pricing calculations that settled you on that pricing plan in the first place. There will be no room for discounting.

One more consideration for determining the price is your market. Most often when calculating an ideal retail price for a product that is needed in a particular region, the process we just went through will land on a retail price that customers will be happy to pay. Even so, it is a good idea to look at similar products in your area and the price people are happy to pay for them. For Bike Shift Levers, you may have to look at the going price for the very cheaply made shifters that have been the only affordable option until now. You can certainly charge quite a bit more than those because customers will realize they are investing in something that will last them much longer and allow them to do their own repairs.

Set your retail price as high as you can without endangering sales with too high a price. Look at adding even one dollar (or the equivalent in your area) to the minimum retail price you find through the earlier calculation process. Then add the appropriate percentage to the other pricing channels. By doing so you will increase your safety buffer through all three pricing channels and better protect your organization from mishaps and unexpected expenses.

Here's that earlier pricing example with a bit more safety buffer:

- Cost to manufacture, assemble, package and deliver each shift lever: $4.00
- Price to sell to distributors: $6.25
- Wholesale price that retailers pay: $8.50
- Retail price that customers pay: $16.99

Note the use of 99 cents to reach the higher retail price for customers. The loss of the penny per sale will cut into profits, but not as much as it will add to sales. Most people see very little difference between the $16.00 and $16.99 price tags. But a price tag that reads $17.00 seems like a major leap and could chase your customers away. If you discovered that your market will barely tolerate your minimum retail price and yet you want to add such a buffer, this sort of detail will go a long way toward success.

MARKETING

Marketing for your Bike Shift Lever should align with any current marketing you have underway. All of our license partners are required to be incorporated nonprofit NGOs or social enterprises, so take stock of your current promotion channels. You likely have a website, a means to send updates to your members and/or supporters such as an e-newsletter, and in-person activities where you can discuss happenings with your members and partners.

Once you have stockpiled at least one hundred or more Bike Shift Levers that are fully packaged and ready for sale and your foundry continues to produce more, begin tapping these marketing channels with a consistent message and image that inspires people to buy. Offer these promotion materials to your retailers to use as well.

If appropriate to your sales plan, you can even include a list of retailers on your website and in your materials to encourage customers to buy through them.

Create several ways for people to buy your Bike Shift Levers so that once they decide they want to buy, they will find their preferred means without having to search.

Set up an inviting retail area at your foundry or at your organization's office. Display your shift levers on a wall or counter in a way that allows customers to try them out before buying. Keep the display clean with all shifters lined up nicely with a bit of space around them. Avoid bunching them together, which has the effect of making something invisible. Include in this retail sales setup full training of your employees and volunteers regarding sticking to the price, how to record the sale, and what to do with the money.

Also train your sales staff how to present the shift levers to customers looking for such a device. Once your sales staff have opened a discussion with a potential customer and found out that this person is looking for a shift lever, train them to point out attributes along with *why* these attributes fit the customer's needs. Simply telling the customer that the shift lever only has six common parts will not be as interesting as saying: "This shift lever has just six parts so that you can easily repair it yourself and it will last for many years of hard use."

An investment in your website to allow online sales will certainly pay off in the end. Talk to your web designer about adding a store, a shopping cart, and a secure means of accepting credit card payments to deposit into your organization's bank account. With a website store in place, add to your home page a tantalizing blurb about your Bike Shift Levers with a link to your store where they can buy their own.

Beyond your own retail sales space, your website store, and your retailers, find any other affordable sales and marketing channels that work in your area. Set up a booth at farmers' markets, popular fairs, and community events to promote your organization and sell your shifters. In some areas, word of mouth is the best way to market a product. In this case, find some influential people to spread the word for you. Sometimes community bulletin boards are popular. Create an eye-catching flyer about your Bike Shift Levers with clear instructions on where to buy them. Road signs, flags attached to bicycles, stickers, and full-sized posters are all possibilities, if they work where you live. Look around your area and note the most common marketing tools, then invest some of your profits into tapping these promotional channels so you will draw the attention of all of your potential customers.

Add your marketing expenses to your overall budget for your Bike Shift Lever program. This overhead expense will cut into profits for awhile, but it will also bring far more sales than if you had kept your casting operation to yourselves.

One Street will also offer marketing resources to our license partners such as ready-to-print brochures, copy for your website, and eye-catching graphics. We will also list all of our up-to-date license partners on our website along with live links to their website so customers in their area who come to our site can easily find them.

SEEK CUSTOMERS OUTSIDE OF BICYCLING

One important note before we move into the next chapter is that Bike Shift Levers work on many other machines besides bicycles. This lever pulls a cable and holds tension. Many other machines require such a lever for their throttles, chokes, and other cable-activated components. Lawn and yard equipment, small motorcycles, go carts, hovercrafts, and boats are part of the long list of small machines that could use such a lever.

Look around your area for these sorts of machines. Then find retailers and repair shops that deal with them. Chances are you will find several additional wholesale customers this way. Also consider adding this information to your website and other promotional materials to catch the eye of potential retail customers looking for such a lever for their small machine.

Now that you have considered all the basics about succeeding with producing and selling Bike Shift Levers as well as other cast products, we can move on to alternative production methods as well as ways you can expand your operation.

Chapter 6

Production Alternatives and Improvements

Alternative methods for producing Bike Shift Levers, or whatever item you have in mind, can range from altering your foundry and workshop to outsourcing production to an existing foundry or machine shop in your area. Before exploring alternatives, make sure to give your own foundry a try. Until you've put the time into solving your particular barriers, you won't have enough information to compare to alternatives to ensure those alternatives are the best route for what you have in mind. You can always contact us for help working out your unique foundry concerns.

We chose casting as the primary method for producing our Bike Shift Levers because it does not require electricity or any complex machines. People who live in remote areas or inner cities rarely have access to advanced machines or the spare parts needed to repair them. However, anyone can find charcoal, a flowerpot, and a steel container to melt scrap aluminum. Every One Street Components project depends on first ensuring that the least equipped people in the world—those who need durable, affordable bike parts the most—can manufacture our bike parts. By starting with these most important people we ensure that anyone at all can make these parts. But that doesn't mean that you must use casting to produce them.

This chapter will look at various other production methods to help you find the most efficient for your situation. Even if you choose casting, there are many ways to improve production, bring down costs, and increase your profits. Start by stepping back and observing your entire operation and its level of efficiency.

INCREASING FOUNDRY EFFICIENCY

As noted earlier, you will find many designs on the internet for larger furnaces using much larger charcoal containers, powerful blowers, and crucibles that must be handled by two people. You will even find designs on the internet for furnaces that use other sorts of fuel such as gas or fuel oil. These may be interesting if these fuels are cheaper than charcoal in your area.

Find the concepts that fit a reasonable expansion plan and avoid building bigger than you need. The larger you make your furnace, the more dangerous everything will become. You could move from workers carrying drink-sized containers of molten metal to containers that could kill one of them if spilled. Discuss your plans with your team and assess all the budgetary numbers before deciding how big your operation really needs to be. Doubling production of Bike Shift Levers simply means doubling the size of your furnace or adding a second one along with doubling the number of molds you're using. The massive designs found on the internet would increase a basic operation tenfold.

Also look at the jobs each of your workers is doing. If you have one worker sorting aluminum, working the crucible, and pouring, an easy way to increase efficiency without having to add equipment is to add another worker. One worker could then focus on sorting and prepping aluminum while the other fills and watches the crucible, pouring when the metal is ready. Adding a third worker would allow one to work entirely with the scrap, the other to focus on the molten metal, and the third to tend to the molds, release the parts, and prepare them for assembly. Assess the amount of time your mold stands idle. Even adding a night shift could double your operation without having to add any new infrastructure to your foundry.

You will also need workers to assemble the parts. In a small operation, these could be the same workers as those working in the foundry as long as the number of shift levers they are producing keeps pace with your orders. One day they could do the casting, the next could be for assembly. Such a setup might be desirable as it would give your workers more variety and offer a break from the heat and smoke of the furnace.

But if orders start to exceed the number of shifters your workers can produce, you will need to hire more workers and perhaps invest in more foundry equipment. Talk with your team to find out if specializing in foundry or assembly sounds like the way to go. By adding workers who focus entirely on assembly, your foundry workers could focus on casting every day.

WORKER COMFORT AND MORALE

Alterations and improvements can go well beyond increasing your furnace size, adding molds, and hiring more workers. Improving your work environment can often increase efficiency far more than adding new equipment. Happy workers who are proud to work for you will stay with you for many years. Not only will these people become your friends and a vital part of your organization, you will save enormous amounts of time and money not having to train new workers.

Observe these precious people, how they move about their work and how they rest. Can you improve their safety and comfort? Are your buildings large enough to allow all your workers to do their jobs well and in comfort? Look at lighting, note temperatures. Furnace work outside in a hot climate can become very uncomfortable if not downright dangerous. Consider setting up a shaded rest area with cold drinks and a water mister where they can relax during breaks and bring their body temperatures back to normal. Perhaps shift your working hours to cooler times of the day. Observe your workers who are assembling the parts. Are their seats comfortable with back support? Are all their tools in good shape and in easy reach? Is lighting excellent so their eyes are not strained? Small investments in simple things like seat cushions, shade areas, and good lighting will pay off over time.

Take careful note of morale as well. Health and safety are not the only things that keep workers happy and productive. Add fun breaks and play. Toss a Frisbee around or kick a soccer ball into the mix. Make sure everyone knows you're making products that will bring joy to people and that joy starts with all of you. Take care of your workers and they will be proud to work hard to produce quality products.

ALTERNATIVE PRODUCTION METHODS

You may wonder if all of this effort of setting up a foundry and caring for workers is right for you. After having read about the intricacies of casting you may decide that messing with molten metal is not your thing. Don't despair. There are many other ways to produce Bike Shift Levers, some are mentioned below. You can still become one of our license partners if you can show us that your alternative production method will result in quality shift levers.

During the license agreement process you will have to provide a sample of a similar part using your proposed machine or foundry in your area (we will only support local manufacturing; that is, manufacturing close to the partner). Then, in order to retain the license, you will have to provide a sample Bike Shift Lever each year from a recent production just as all license partners have to do. Look through the Resources section of this book, scan the internet, and talk to local metal workers to get a full picture of the alternatives available to you.

Going the DIY route opens up a whole different realm of possibilities because you won't have to stick to the exacting standards required of our license partners. Doing it yourself to make just a few for your own needs, you can discover many creative ways to make the lever and base of the Bike Shift Lever. With patience, these parts could be carved from hardwood, bone, or even a soft stone. A skilled potter may even find success using ceramics, though the resultant shift levers would be more fragile than their original design intended. Still, personalizing your Bike Shift Levers with artful style has no limit. If one method doesn't last long, that gives you a chance to try another.

Study the drawings in Appendix B before you begin. Aligning the cable and bolt holes are the most critical details. Beyond that, you could have lots of fun customizing your own pair of shift levers. The lever could be made longer or taller, carved into animal shapes, perhaps teeth or a tail. Notches or nubs could be added to the hard material for attaching add-ons like rubber grip material or dangling items to customize your ride. While such alterations would not be allowed for the Bike Shift

Levers made and sold by our license partners, as long as you are only making a few for your own use, there are no limits to the fun you can have playing with the design and production methods you want to try.

3D PRINTING

If you have a 3D printer or know someone or a shop with one, you can try printing out each of these parts in plastic. We will not accept plastic parts from license partners because plastic is not durable enough to serve the needs of people who rely on their bicycles every day. Plastic also degrades in sunlight. But if you are doing this only DIY for yourself, give it a try. The beauty of 3D printing is it allows you to try out alternative designs with just a few adjustments on the screen. The printer does all the rest. In fact, a 3D printer might be a convenient way for you to test your creative designs before investing time in carving or forming various materials.

Someday 3D printers may finally evolve into affordable metal printing. At that point we will be happy to inspect parts made from a 3D metal printer for potential licensing as long as the price per shifter would be comparable to the cast price. Of course, even if printed in metal by a 3D printer, anyone hoping to license with us to manufacture one of our bike parts will still have to follow our design and requirements—not as much fun as the DIY route has to offer.

OUTSOURCING TO A LOCAL FOUNDRY

One of the easiest alternatives is to find a foundry near you and pay them to do the casting. You will have to pay them a lot more money than you would have spent using your own foundry, but you also get to skip all the set up costs and hassles. If you are a license partner, they can use the permanent mold you receive with your agreement. Before you contract with them, take the time to ask about and note every cost they will charge you for each part. Then run all your budget numbers to ensure your cost per part and the price at which you can sell them in your area will continue to bring you a profit over time.

Going the DIY route, local foundries will often use sand casting or lost wax for such short run, specialty jobs. They will need one of each of the parts in order to create a pattern that they will then use to create the mold. They will also likely want to see the drawings in Appendix B to ensure that the pattern they make will result in a close replica.

If you choose to work with an outside foundry, they will charge you for their time to either use your mold or create the patterns, set up sand molds, and pour each of the parts you request. They will also charge you retail price for the metal. Working with an outside foundry also adds the cost of your time to check their work at every step including the pattern they create and the result of a test pour using that pattern.

These costs could make a lot of sense for someone only needing a few made for their own use. On the other hand, the costs of working with an outside foundry to produce Bike Shift Levers could add up over time and cut deeply into your potential profits. Be sure to calculate all of this before choosing an outside foundry for your production method.

CNC MACHINING

Computer Numerical Control (CNC) machining is another alternative for producing the parts. It starts with advanced Computer Aided Design (CAD) software that records every measurement of the item you want to make. This design is then entered into a Computer Aided Manufacture (CAM) program, which translates this information to the CNC cutting and milling machine. The machinist simply places a block of base metal into the machine and turns on the switch. Then the machine cuts and shapes that block according to the directions given by the software.

You may have your own CNC machine or can hire a machine shop to make the parts. For Bike Shift Levers, the drawings in Appendix B should give an experienced CAD designer enough information to create such a program for their particular CNC machine. Once the machine knows what to cut, the machinist can let it do the work.

We do not recommend that our license partners use CNC machining to make Bike Shift Levers because the price of each shift lever will have to be so much higher than ones made by casting in order to cover all the costs. This process requires starting with clean blocks of aluminum, also called billet, which you or your machinist would purchase at a metal supplier in your area. Of course purchasing new aluminum will come with a much greater cost than collecting scrap. The costs of the cutting tools and running the machine are also quire high. These added costs will increase the cost of each shift lever and raise the retail price you must set in order to make even a slight profit. The up side is that you will know exactly which aluminum alloy you are working with. Something in the 2xxx, 6xxx or 7xxx series would be ideal for the CNC process because of their good machining qualities.

The high costs of running these fancy machines, replacing their cutting bits, and purchasing the new, billet aluminum add up quick. This is why, even if you license with us, we will only supply a casting mold. If you still choose to produce your Bike Shift Levers using CNC machining, you will need to create that program yourself. Even so, with your own machine, a cheap source of billet aluminum, and lots of experience with CNC, you might still find that this method actually works best for your needs. For someone trying the DIY route, who already has their own CNC machine and the patience to set up the program, making a few this way might be worth the time and effort.

Start by noting all the costs of your chosen production method before you move ahead. With CNC, you will have to include the cost to convert the drawings into CAD, the cost of the billet, the cost of the machine shop, and the cost of your time to ensure quality parts result.

OUTSOURCING CONCERNS

No matter the process used, when working with an outside foundry or machine shop, start with a written agreement that includes your inspection and approval of the first test run of parts produced before they move into full production. You do not want to join the long list of unhappy customers who outsourced their casting or machine work only to pay for the delivery of hundreds if not thousands of useless parts that had to be thrown away.

This brings up just one of the many reasons why we do not encourage outsourcing to another country for your parts manufacturing. Horror stories of prepayments made for boxes of useless parts are just one direct reason to avoid it.

Outsourcing to other countries also undermines every principle behind the Bike Shift Lever project. On the surface, the monetary savings seem logical. Because of this, suggestions to outsource production of Bike Shift Levers to foreign factories have come to us since the beginning, but always from people who have not taken the time to learn what this project is about. As you read in the

Preface, this project is responding to a growing need from our partners around the world who are in need of simple, affordable, quality bicycle parts to better serve the bicycle needs of people in their communities. These organizations not only provide bikes, they also help their neighbors build careers with bicycles so they can lift themselves out of poverty. By keeping production and all of its accompanying infrastructure in their community, these organizations are building a system that combats poverty for many generations to come.

Outsourcing to another country would eliminate these benefits. Boxes of Bike Shift Levers would arrive. No career training in production. No salary for production workers. No local facility to support their employees and eventually expand into making other bike parts and perhaps even whole bicycles. Plus, the people in that community could never point to a bike part or bicycle and say, "I made that."

From the other perspective, factories that manufacture products to be shipped away, often abuse their workers with long hours, terrible working conditions, and low wages. Their workers never enjoy the use of the parts they spend their days making. Many of these factories also engage in environmentally destructive practices that go unchecked by the environmental standards held by the home countries of those ordering the parts. Every order to such a factory reinforces those practices and encourages them to continue.

Your foundry operation is also susceptible to cutting corners and doing harm. Your production volume would never come close to the volume of items produced by these factories. Even so, make every effort to engage proper environmental practices—keep toxic fumes to a minimum by seeking mostly unpainted scrap and avoid charcoal made from old-growth or endangered trees. Also, take great care to ensure the safety and wellbeing of your workers. By establishing these beneficial practices, you will build a strong reputation in your community that will help build your business for the long term.

BENEFITS OF LOCAL PRODUCTION

In nearly every industry around the world a cry to bring production back to the local level is growing. Locally grown food is at the forefront. Local breweries are taking off in the United States. Even local manufacturing of clothing, furniture, and toys are becoming popular. More and more shoppers are choosing to pay a bit more in order to support companies where their neighbors work. One website, SFMade.org, is an interesting example of a community coming together to support their own local manufacturers, this one in San Francisco. MadeinNYC.org is another, similar site for New York City. The DIY and maker movements offer support systems to encourage entrepreneurs to design and manufacture their products locally.

At One Street Components, we are creating a similar support system, but focused entirely on the bicycle industry. By supporting local production of bikes and parts, we are also empowering local organizations to learn the metal craft that once made the bicycle a simple, elegant machine. Once they have the means to produce even a few important bike parts, perhaps even just Bike Shift Levers, these organizations will begin to loosen the grip of dependence held by just a few massive bike companies. These companies are either entirely focused on high-end racing and expensive designer bikes or pumping out useless bicycle-shaped objects that are hardly rideable. The parts and bicycles made by these companies have little relevance to the vast majority of the world's population. As mentioned earlier, eighty percent of the people living on this planet live in or near poverty. These people either already ride their bike every day or wish they had a simple, durable bike they could depend on and repair themselves. They don't need lightweight fragile parts that cost them a month's salary. They need simple, affordable parts that will hold up for many years of hard use.

Organizations focused on helping people with bicycles and bicycle careers are also struggling because they can no longer find simple, durable bikes or repair parts. They should not have to compromise their principles and waste untold, precious funding on bicycles and parts that will not hold up to the rigorous needs of the people they are trying to help, who rely on their bike every day.

Beyond the immediate urgency of serving the needs of impoverished people, most anyone who rides a bike will appreciate these simple, durable bike parts. Racers aside, most people like knowing that the bike part they are purchasing will hold up for many years and, once it begins to wear, can be repaired easily and affordably. Knowing that the bike part they just purchased was made by one of their neighbors will make them all the more proud to support their local bike part manufacturer. As local production of bikes and parts finally returns, throwaway bike parts made in far-off lands will no longer be the only option available, and will certainly not be the most desirable.

Local production can go well beyond bike parts and the few other pioneering locally manufactured products appearing these days. By learning these basic production steps outlined in this book, readers can go on to design and produce other bike parts and products outside the bike industry. Just knowing that you can turn a pile of scrap aluminum into something useful should give you the confidence to try your hand at other designs and even learn other crafts such as blacksmithing, CNC machining, and welding. Let your creativity flow!

SEND US YOUR STORIES

At One Street Components we are already looking ahead to the next bike parts we'll design and manufacture. We're listening for requests from our partner organizations for the most urgent bike parts needed. Bike Shift Levers are only our first. Let us know what bike parts have been driving you crazy with their complexity, price, and inability to be repaired. Bike chains are already on our radar as the big companies move toward chains that cannot be repaired with a chain tool or hammer and nail, as is common in many remote areas. Rear derailleurs have also made our list as partners who need Bike Shift Levers point out that the derailleurs they will be shifting are not holding up to their customers' needs.

The bike industry's move toward disc brakes makes us wonder whether simple cantilever brakes will start to disappear just as simple, quality shift levers vanished. Their addition of new wheel and tire sizes is also complicating things. Send us your thoughts on the next most likely simple bike parts to be added to the endangered list.

We'd also love to hear about your experiences using this book to cast Bike Shift Levers or anything else. Any changes or modifications you made to the furnace or the sorts of molds you used could make fun material for our blog posts and perhaps even the next edition of this book. If you discover ways to improve on the Bike Shift Lever design or use it to move on to other bike part designs we'd love to hear about it. Our learning curve has been steep since we started and we don't expect it to level off anytime soon. Your ideas and experiences will help us discover even better ways to proceed as we seek out ways to bring simple, locally manufactured bikes and parts back to the world. Please send your stories, thoughts, comments, and ideas to:

One Street Components
P.O. Box 3309
Prescott, AZ 86302 USA
info@onestreet.org

Have fun with all of your designing, casting, and crafting of items that help people or simply inspire them to look beyond mass-produced products. The more people who take on local manufacturing, the better our world will be. Thank you!

Appendix A

Aluminum Alloys and Common Uses

Alloy Series	Major Alloying Elements and Their Characteristics	Common Uses
1xxx	**None** - 99% minimum aluminum, soft, easy to weld and shape, but lacks strength	Thin foil, sheet, and plate
2xxx	**Copper (max. 7%)** – adds good strength, but hinders weldability; heat treatable	Plate, extruded tube and rod; sometimes forged; rarely cast or sheet; screws, rivets, fasteners, structural and automotive parts
3xxx (wrought)	**Manganese (max. 2%)** – adds medium strength; improves weldability, corrosion resistance and formability	Sheet and plate; sometimes extruded; beverage can bodies, tanks, cooking utensils, rain gutters
3xxx (cast)	**Silicon (max. 23%) + Copper (max. 5%) and/or Magnesium (max. 1%)** – Silicon adds fluidity for casting, others add strength; heat treatable	Most common alloy for production casting especially automotive
4xxx	**Silicon (max. 14%)** – adds medium strength; lowers melting point and increases fluidity; only some are heat treatable	Often used for production casting
5xxx	**Magnesium (max. 6%)** – adds good strength, salt water corrosion resistance; improves weldability, but hinders heat treatability	Sheet and plate; rarely cast; most common for marine uses, also tanks and tops of beverage cans
6xxx	**Magnesium (max. 2%) + Silicon (max. 2%)** – retains medium strength and good weldability of 5xxx, adds heat treatability	Most used for extrusions – tube, rod, shaped; also forged, sheet, and plate; bridges, trusses, window frames, ladders, bike frames, forged crank arms, other bike parts
7xxx	**Zinc (max. 8%)** – adds significant strength, heat treatability, but more vulnerable to corrosion	Plate, forged and extruded rod and tube; rarely cast; bike frames, other bike parts, aircraft and motorcycle parts
8xxx	**Tin, Lithium & other elements (various percentages)** – high conductivity	Specialty items such as bearings, bushings, cables and wire

Appendix B

Bike Shift Lever Part Drawing
LEVER

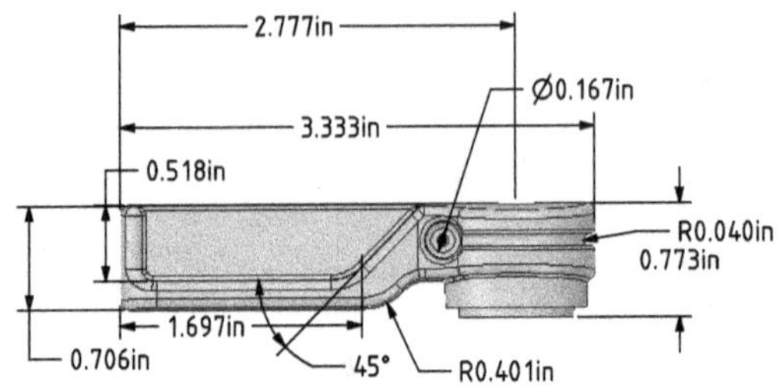

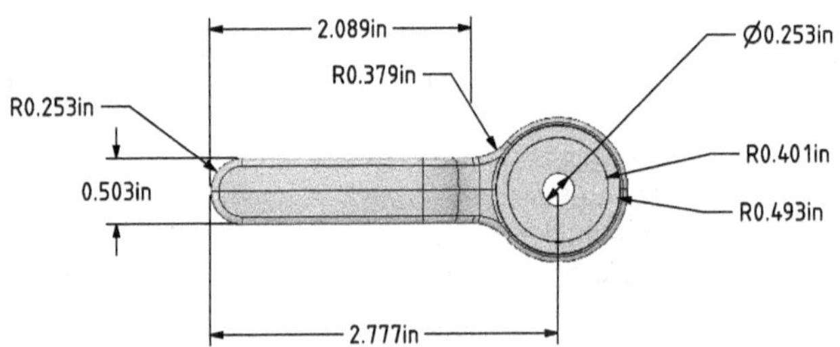

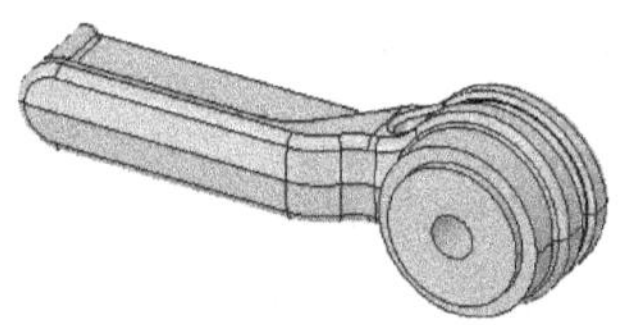

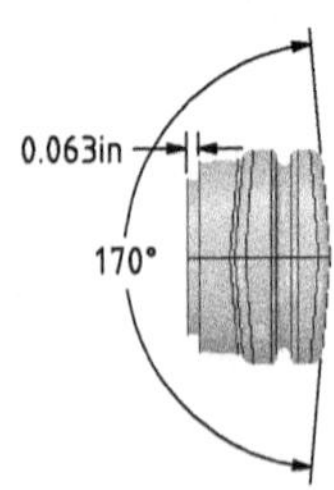

Appendix B

Bike Shift Lever Part Drawing
BASE

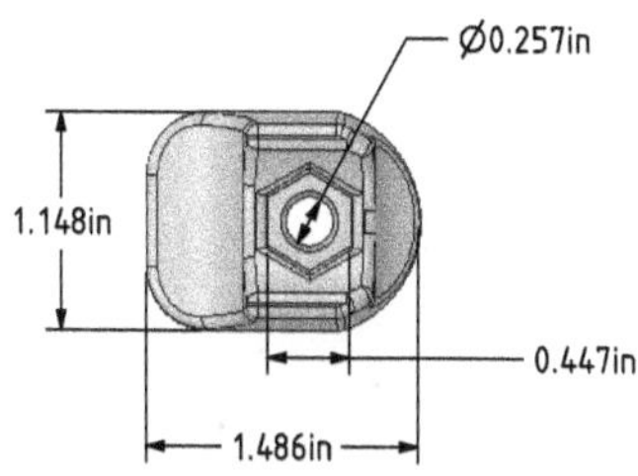

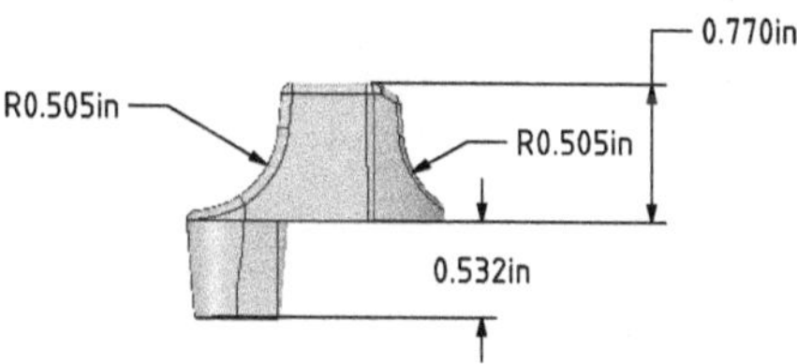

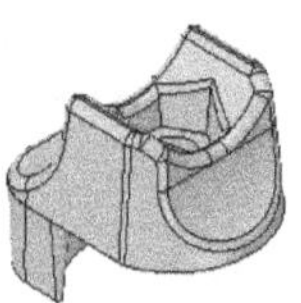

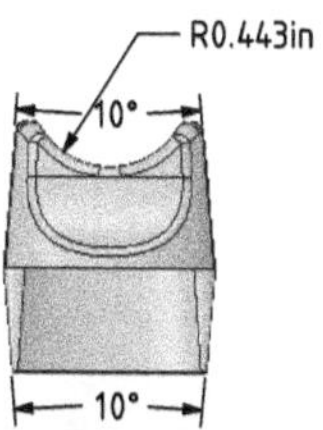

Resources and References

BOOKS

- *Casting Aluminum*, Reynolds Metals Company, 1965
- *Defying Poverty with Bicycles*, Sue Knaup, One Street Press, 2012
- *The Disappearing Spoon,* Sam Kean, Back Bay Books, 2010
- *Handbook of Aluminum,* George E. Totten, Marcel Dekker, 2003
- *Melting and Casting Aluminum*, Robert J. Anderson, Baird & Co., 1925
- *Metal Casting*, Steve Hurst, Intermediate Technology Publications, 1996

WEB RESOURCES

- "Aluminium and Aluminium Alloys – Designations," http://www.azom.com/article.aspx?ArticleID=310
- *European Cycling Lexicon* – translations of bicycle parts, tools, and other terms into 27 languages; find link on OneStreet.org under Resources, Bike Shops
- iFixit.org – articles and resources for repairing and reusing items
- Makerspace.com – community spaces with shared prototyping tools
- Makezine.com – Maker and DIY projects
- OneStreet.org – find Bike Shift Lever details under Programs, One Street Components

Acknowledgements

This book would not have been possible without the many helpers who offered their time and expertise from the very beginning, when the Bike Shift Lever was only an idea.

Dick Hartley stands out as an important helper in the early design stages. He is also one of the top contributors to the project as he donated all of his time. Dick worked with Sue Knaup to transfer her rough design drawings into CAD and CNC programs to produce the first prototypes of the shift lever in aluminum. Dick's CAD drawings enabled the mold design and thus opened the way for the project to proceed to completion.

Sue Knaup not only designed the Bike Shift Lever, but spent countless hours seeking helpers and compiling our lessons learned into this book.

Laura Zeman-Mullen, our patent attorney for the Bike Shift Lever, contributed her time and expertise in order to assist the project. Without Laura, we would have made many costly mistakes and could not have afforded to patent the shift lever.

Clint Brown, One Street's pro-bono attorney, also

contributed legal advice that guided us into Laura's care.

Russ Cummings, CEO of Tool Exchange, and Jim Stein, CEO of J.A. Stein Company, both offered valuable insight regarding parts choices for the shift levers. Their understanding of common hardware sizes and availability helped shape the final design. Russ was also one of the proofreaders of this book noting where more clarity was needed. Jim also worked with Sue to design the jig for finishing the cast parts.

Dan Depaemelaere of Wheels Manufacturing deserves our thanks for advising Sue on the intricacies of rapid prototyping and 3D printing. This knowledge was invaluable in the search for an appropriate prototype machinist and ultimately led Sue to Dick Hartley.

Michael Linke has assisted in many areas of this project. Because he and his organization, Bicycling Empowerment Network Namibia, will likely be one of our first license partners, Michael has offered this important perspective. Michael also serves as a One Street Advisor and served as our Secretary/Treasurer during the year we completed this book and moved into production. In this role Michael contributed countless hours of guidance, proofreading, and discussion as we developed the project.

Other One Street Advisors who contributed significant time include Kaethi Diethelm, Karen Nozik, and Jim Knaup who all offered ideas and insight during the early stages. Morten Kerr served as Vice President as the project came to fruition, offering important guidance and feedback. Paul Simpson, Justin Hyatt, and Jerry Hiniker also took the time to read through critical parts of the book and suggest improvements.

The project would have been dead in the water by the end of 2013 if not for the 175 generous donors who contributed through our Kickstarter campaign to fund the final production costs and publication of this book. Many of these enthusiastic donors also took the time to offer ideas and improvements for the project. Several also stepped up to serve as testers of the very first shift levers. Robert Milligan created our Kickstarter video that helped attract these critical donors.

Ross Evans of Xtracycle and Worldbike (a top Kickstarter supporter) provided insight from his experience developing Xtracycle's license guidelines. Very few bicycle products encourage entrepreneurial licensing, so Ross's expertise was a great help in our license development process.

As we moved into mold design, we realized we'd entered an entirely new world. For five long months Sue sought a machine shop willing to design and produce the molds. During that frustrating time, casting experts in Prescott, including Ed Williman, Michael Meyers (who also proofread this book), Doug Wilson, and Ralph Simpson all contributed valuable expertise. Ed especially spent long hours assessing the mold design needs to ensure that both shifter parts were properly fed with aluminum. Michael continues to offer ideas for expanding the project into the future.

When the hunt for a machine shop hit a dead end, Aaron Wieler stepped in to design the mold in CAD and produce drawings that most machine shops could work from. Aaron returned to assist as a proofreader of this book, offering his insight from his experience designing useful bicycles and other vehicles for developing countries.

Aaron's drawings enabled Sue to reach beyond common machine shops and through this outreach, connected with Chris Nurre, CEO of BikeFitKit. Initially Chris believed he could machine the molds, but after many attempts with his machine, realized he did not have the right setup.

Chris introduced Sue to CNC Prose in Salt Lake City and that is when the blockage broke. CNC Prose thrives on mold making. Andy Martin, the machinist we work with there, was actually thrilled by the challenge and contributed much of his time simply because he appreciates the goals of this project.

Besides the proofreaders noted above, Joe and Connie Breeze read the draft with care. Joe went at it from his bicycle design experience, noting spots that needed more technical detail. Connie went at it from her copyediting experience, helping to smooth out the first part of the book in particular.

Every one of these helpers was critical to the progress of this project. Had any of them dropped the ball, we would have faced more frustrating delays. We can't thank them enough for their selfless contributions, patience, and willingness to see their contribution through. We hope they know how valuable they have been to bringing the Bike Shift Lever and this book to the world.

Index

E

F

H

I

J

L

M

N

O

P

R

S

T

W

Z

www.ingramcontent.com/pod-product-compliance
Lightning Source LLC
Chambersburg PA
CBHW072203090426
42740CB00012B/2368
* 9 7 8 0 9 8 5 9 8 8 9 1 3 *